AKBAR

AKBAR
From a contemporary drawing in the India Office Library

AKBAR

By
SIR LAURENCE BINYON

NEW YORK
D. APPLETON AND COMPANY
1932

TO
WILLIAM ROTHENSTEIN
A LOVER OF INDIA
IN TOKEN OF OLD FRIENDSHIP

I am indebted to my friend and colleague, J. V. S. Wilkinson, for correcting the proofs, and to my wife for compiling the Index.

L. B.

AKBAR

I

CONTEMPLATING the favourites of Fame (whose
laurel is bestowed, like Fortune's smile, not
always according to desert), mankind is wil-
lingly credulous. Magnified by time and distance, these far-seen personages gather round
them an air of fable. Sometimes, conscious of
their power to hallucinate, they have conspired
with the world's credulity to create their own
legend. In vain are the efforts of the rational,
when once a man possesses the imagination of
the world. All the exposed littlenesses and
falsifications of a Napoleon fail to prevent him
from towering over his time.

But in Akbar, one of the world's great conquerors, and a greater ruler, there is something
which spontaneously rejects the legendary. It
is true that his historians have dutifully made
some little attempts to surround him with a
superhuman glory. The usual portents are
said to have occurred: at seven months the baby
made an eloquent speech from the cradle. But
the fictitious aureole fails to cling. It is as if
the man himself shook off such fetters with im-

1

patience. Not that he had no appetite for glory; far from it. But the reality, he would have felt, sufficed.

Akbar was the grandson of that joyous and superb adventurer Babur, who, inheriting the throne of a small, though delectable, country in the middle of Asia, spent his life in fighting and scheming for a grander throne; he ended by swooping down on Hindostan and conquering there a great dominion. His son Humayun held this precariously till he was driven out by rival rulers of Afghan race; after years of exile he won back his throne, only to die. Humayun's son, Akbar, then but a boy, had to fight for his inheritance. He secured it; and then, piece by piece, kingdom by kingdom, he annexed in an almost incessant series of wars the countries surrounding his frontiers, till his empire stretched from sea to sea. Except for that southern portion of India called the Deccan, he became master of India.

Such was his achievement as conqueror. His greater achievement as a ruler was to weld this collection of different states, different races, different religions, into a whole. It was accomplished by elaborate organisation—Akbar had an extraordinary genius for detail—still more by the settled policy which persuaded his

2

subjects of the justice of their ruler. Akbar's conceptions were something new in the history of Asiatic conquerors. Though a foreigner, he identified himself with the India he had conquered. And much of his system was to be permanent. The principles and practice worked out by Akbar and his ministers were largely adopted into the English system of government.

Yet Akbar's achievements are transcended in interest by the man himself. And in a little book like the present it is the portrait of the man rather than the story of his doings with which we shall be most concerned. The full record of his conquests and administration can be read in the pages of Mr. Vincent Smith's *Akbar, the Great Mogul*: a volume which has its faults and which is sometimes curiously unjust to its hero, but in which is collected a vast amount of solid information. The chief original authority is the *Akbar-namah,* the *Story of Akbar,* written in Persian by the emperor's friend and minister, Abul Fazl. There are other Indian histories. But of greater interest to us, perhaps, are the vivid accounts given by the Jesuits who stayed at Akbar's court and sometimes accompanied him on his expeditions.

Hardly any one so conspicuously eminent in

3

history is so plainly set before our eyes or has so actual a presence in our imagination. The detailed records of his daily life, no less than of his achievements, are corroborated not only by numerous portraits but by a long series of small paintings (English collectors have brought home a great number of these), in which his manifold activities are vividly depicted. We have him before our eyes in his prime of life. He is compact of frame, muscular, rather burly; of moderate stature, but broad-shouldered; neither lean nor stout; of a healthy complexion, the colour of ripe wheat. His eyes, rather small, but with long lashes, sparkle like the points of light on little waves when they catch the sun. He wears moustaches, but no beard. His voice is loud and full. When he laughs, it is with his whole face. His movements are quick, though from much riding in his youth he is slightly bow-legged. He carries his head a little on one side over the right shoulder. His nose is no commanding beak; it is straight and small, the nostrils wide and mobile. Below the left nostril is a wart, thought to be very agreeable in appearance. In whatever assemblage of men, he is recognisably the king. He radiates energy. His temper is naturally violent; and he is aware of it, so much so, that his orders are that no death-warrant is to be carried out till it is twice confirmed. His anger is terrible, but easily appeased. He has an insatiable curiosity, and loves new things. His mind is as incessantly employed as his body.

And yet strange to say, Akbar, the greatest and, except possibly Philip of Spain, the wealthiest potentate of his time in the world, a man versed in history and poetry and delighting in philosophical discussion, is illiterate. He can neither read nor write. It is true that there exists on the flyleaf of a precious manuscript copy of the 'Life of Timur,' Akbar's ancestor, a single signature of his, laboriously written in a childish hand and reverently attested by his son Jahangir. But this signature, preserved as an unique marvel, only confirms the universal testimony to his inability. Yet, if unable to read, he is all the more able to remember. He has books read aloud to him, and knows them better than if he had read them himself. His memory indeed is as prodigious as his energy.

A traveller from Europe in the latter part of the sixteenth century who should arrive at last in the Mogul's dominion would find no difficulty in seeing the emperor at close quarters and enjoying his conversation. Foreigners were welcome; and indeed among those who habitually thronged the courtyards at Fatehpur-Sikri, that strange splendid city built at Akbar's whim and afterwards so suddenly abandoned, were men of various Asiatic races, predominantly Persians, Turks, and Hindus, and of many divers creeds. 'The Great Mogul' was a sort of fairy-tale in the West; yet here were all the marks of a civilisation closely parallel with that of Europe, though so different on the surface. The external magnificence might have some touches of the barbaric; but then what barbarities mingled with the refinements of European courts! What dirt was disguised by the perfumes! Refinements were here of every sort: not only luxurious appointments and the gratification of the senses, but a love of letters and the arts. Poetry was held in high honour, and the ingenuity of the Persian poets' 'conceits' could rival those of Marini and his northern imitators. Painters and architects abounded, under the direct patronage of the emperor, who himself had learnt to draw and was a skilled musician, besides being a worker in half a dozen handicrafts. If theological disputation and religious animosities were a sign of high civilisation, these rivalled in fierceness

6

those of Western countries; but while in Europe
the disputants burnt or massacred one another
in their zeal, and devastated whole countries in
the name of religion, here in India a restrain-
ing power prevented arguments from ending in
the use of swords: here was a monarch who
actually believed in toleration.

Any day, then, our traveller might have seen
Akbar holding a reception; for he holds audience twice a day. The blaze of the Indian sun
makes strong shadows from the verandah-pillars
of the red sandstone palace, where Akbar
receives one courtier or envoy after another.
Peacocks sun themselves on the roof of the verandah; in the courtyard elephants are slowly
led; a groom holds a cheetah in leash; an animated crowd of virile-looking men in dresses
of fine silk and of various colours stand about.
Akbar himself is dressed in a surcoat reaching
to the knees (were he a stricter Muslim it
would reach to the feet), and wears a closely-
rolled turban hiding his hair; a rope of great
pearls hangs from his neck. His manner has
subtle changes. With the great he is great and
does not unbend; to the humble he is kindly
and sympathetic. It is noticeable how he makes
more of the small presents of the poor (and he
is very fond of presents) than of the costly gifts

of the nobles, at which he will hardly glance. As a dispenser of justice he is famous; every one wronged (an observer has said) 'believes the emperor is on his side.'

Four times in twenty-four hours Akbar prays to God: at sunrise, at noon, at sunset, and midnight. But any one who tried to keep up with his daily activities would need to be of iron make. Three hours suffice for Akbar's sleep. He eats but one meal a day, and that at no fixed time. He eats but little meat, less and less as he grows older: 'Why should we make ourselves a sepulchre for beasts?' is one of his sayings. Rice and sweetmeats are the chief of his diet, and fruit, of which he is extremely fond. His day is a long one, and he fills it full. Between state councils and conferences with ministers or generals he inspects his elephants—of which he has five thousand in his stables—his horses, and other animals. He knows them by name. He notes their condition; if any show signs of growing thin and poorly, the keeper responsible finds his salary docked. Presently he will repair to an upper terrace where are the dove-cotes, built of blue and white brick, and with infinite pleasure he watches the evolutions of the tumbler-pigeons, deploying and returning, massing or separating, to the sound of a whistle. Part of the day is devoted to the harem, in which there are three hundred women. At another time he will be watching (like Marcus Aurelius) gladiatorial combats, or fights between elephants, or between elephants and lions. But though entering with such zest on his amusements, his mind is occupied also with other things: for messengers arrive continually from every part of the empire and rapid decisions have to be taken. Another time he is inspecting his school of painters, passing quickly among them and appraising their work. Or he will go down to the workshop, and turn carpenter or stonemason. He is especially fond of the foundry, and loves to found a cannon with his own hands.

When at evening lights are lit in the great hall, the emperor takes his seat among his courtiers and has books read to him; or music is played, and Akbar himself joins in or he laughs at jests and stories. If there are foreigners present, he plies them with unceasing questions. He will sit far into the night absorbed in discussions on religion: this is one of his dear delights. He drinks wine, or wine mixed with opium, and sometimes falls into a stupor: but this does not affect his terrible energy. Yet this crowded, pulsing life does not wholly absorb

9

him. Frequently he will disappear and sit apart in solitary meditation for hours at a time.

Such is Akbar's way of life at court. But these are only intervals between campaigns, which he always opens with a hunt on an enormous scale. Even on his campaigns he will, when there is no need for swift marching, pursue much the same occupations.

Of how many notable people in the world's history does our knowledge seem so complete?

Yet do we really, after all, know Akbar the man? What is the truth about his character? Quite contrary opinions have been expressed; and many of his actions can be interpreted in opposite ways.

Since the witness of Akbar's own historian, Abul Fazl, may be thought too prejudiced—he is indeed fulsome in flattery, though he records with equanimity acts which, to us at any rate, are not very creditable—let us turn to the Jesuits; they certainly had no motive for giving Akbar more than his due.

'He never,' says Bartoli, 'gave anybody the chance to understand rightly his inmost sentiments or to know what faith or religion he held by, but in whatever way he could best serve his own interests he used to feed one party or the other with the hope of gaining

him to itself, humouring each side with fair
words. A man apparently free from guile, as
honest and candid as could be imagined, but
in reality so close and self-contained, with twists
of words and deeds so divergent from each
other and most times so contradictory, that even
by much seeking one could not find the clue
to his thoughts.'

That is one view: the portrait of a consum-
mate dissembler, open in appearance, inwardly
subtle and deceitful and bent only on his own
aggrandisement. And if this clue be accepted,
it is easy to read Akbar's actions in that light.
When he is humane to an enemy or traitor—
and his humanity seemed extraordinary to his
contemporaries—he can be represented as
humane only from policy. And his wars of ag-
gression, which some have represented to have
been undertaken from the noblest motives only,
have been pictured by others as merely the behaviour of 'a pike in pond, preying on its
weaker neighbours.' In fact, the truth about
Akbar is not simple; his was by nature a complex character; in the intricacy of circumstances
its complexity was bound to be increased. But
let us try to approach it a little closer.

The Jesuits came into contact with Akbar
through discussions on religion. He had sent

for them of his own accord, and they had hoped to convert him. But they had every excuse for being exasperated with him, since he always in the end eluded their grasp, and nothing is more natural than Bartoli's angry outburst. But when the question of religion is in abeyance, when the ground is neutral and there is no occasion for prejudice, we find a different tone.

'*The king is by nature simple and straightforward.*' These are the words of the Jesuit Monserrate, who accompanied Akbar on his Kabul expedition; and the occasion was the discovery by Akbar of treachery on the part of a man he had loaded with honours. 'Naturally humane, gentle and kind' is the phrase of Peruschi. 'Just to all men,' says another.

'By nature simple and straightforward': that, I think, is the truth; but we must stress a little that '*by nature.*' For, that a man should live the life led by Akbar, accomplish what he accomplished, and succeed in being always simple and straightforward, would be something of a miracle. In continual danger from his boyhood, he was surrounded by treachery, jealousy, and intrigue. He seldom knew whom he could trust. He had continually to wear a mask and to hide his thoughts in self-defence. The astonishing thing is that he did not end in protecting himself by an armour of permanent suspicion and guile, but that he would often trust men after they had proved unfaithful, still seeking to find 'if any portion of good remains in that evil nature,' as he said on one occasion. But was he to be trusted himself? Not perhaps when ambition possessed him, or a great scheme was at stake. We shall find, when we come to recount them, certain events in which he cannot be acquitted of unscrupulous and even perfidious behaviour. And yet fundamentally, I am persuaded, he was honest and sincere. See how, when he meets a transparently honest nature, like Ridolfo Aquaviva, the mutual liking is instinctive.

'Naturally humane and kind.' Every one was struck by this aspect of Akbar's character, remarkable indeed in one who had the absolute powers of an autocrat and who suffered so much from faithless servants. Yet he could be fiercely cruel in his anger. Historians are accustomed to condone the faults of a great man by arguing that they were the faults of his time. But a man shows his greatness by the measure in which he surpasses the standards of his age. Akbar's acts of cruelty, less cold-blooded than the cruelties of contemporary rulers in Europe

—and even twentieth-century Europe cannot afford to give itself superior airs in this respect —these acts shock us because they were done by Akbar, who could be so singularly generous and forgiving. Akbar said, 'The noblest quality of princes is the forgiveness of faults.' And his kindness and humanity are the more surprising in one who had in his veins the blood of the two most pitiless conquerors the world has known, Jinghiz Khan and Tamerlane. Vincent Smith maintains that Akbar's clemency in his earlier years was merely policy; that if he had been strong enough he would have punished and not spared. Who shall say? Motives mingle. But if he perceived that the humane course was not only generous but sensible, I think we should rather admire his intelligence than blame his astuteness.

At any rate, Akbar's clemency, like Caesar's, was famous. Was he also, like Caesar, an epileptic? The native historians say nothing of it, nor does Monserrate, the Jesuit, who knew him intimately. The statement that he had the falling sickness is casually made in Du Jarric's compilation from Jesuit notes and records, on what authority is unknown, and only there. The Jesuits supposed that he took to sports and amusements to distract his melancholy; which seems a superfluous conjecture. But the fact of the disease is not improbable. Akbar's second son Murad developed epilepsy.

'Just to all men.' It was Akbar's justice that chiefly reconciled the peoples he conquered to his rule. It was a basic quality in his nature. And it proceeded not so much, I think, from a sense of law, as from a sort of uncorrupted innocence of mind which persisted through all his experience of the world. Innocence may seem a strange word to use. I mean an innate candour powerful enough to be able to see things unclouded by the prejudices which we absorb from our surroundings or inherit from the past or imbibe from early teaching, and to which most natures unconsciously surrender. There were impositions which for centuries the Muhammadan conquerors had laid upon the Hindus. They had been accepted as things of course. They were the conquerors' due. To Akbar with his direct vision they seemed unjust; and though hardly more than a boy, against all tradition, against the opposition of every one, he abolished them. It was again in the teeth of the most dangerous opposition that he made overtures to the Jesuits and seemed

on the verge of adopting Christianity. What
held him back in the end? It was the thought
to which, with a child's obstinacy, he was always
returning: there are good men professing every
creed, and each proclaiming his creed to be
true, all the others false; how can one be sure
that he is right? He was the antithesis of a
bigot. On the other hand, he was anything
but indifferent. For in this man of action, this
lover of life, whose body exulted in its strength
and who strode through the world so confi-
dently, there was hidden a profound capacity
for sadness, self-doubting thoughts, dissatisfac-
tions, a craving for illumination. From boyhood he had, from time to time, mystical experiences, in which he seemed to be given direct
communion with the Divine Presence; and on
his death-bed, when he was past recognising
men and past all speech, while eager theologians
hung over him in the hope to direct the depart-
ing soul, he was heard murmuring to himself
and endeavouring to articulate the name of
God. So it was that the Jesuit fathers, intent
to win all of him or nothing, supposed him
to be tortuously evading them for some subtle
policy of his own, whereas it was really his own
baffled simplicity of reasoning, never able to
surrender itself to authority from without,

which in its turn baffled them. There is something engaging in Akbar's faults and weaknesses, which were not petty, but rather belonged to the things which made him great. He was, above all things, human.

II

WHAT was Akbar's inheritance? What was the background of his mind?

We have for a moment to forget the European heritage which is in our blood and to which we are so accustomed that we take it for granted: the art, the literature, the philosophy, of Greece, the imperial memory of Rome, Roman law and Roman roads, all the complex tissue of the medieval legacy. In place of them is the Muhammadan culture, not wholly separated from ours, since Islam derives so much from Judaism and Christianity and, through Arab writers, from Greece, but in art and letters looking always to the classics of Iran: Persian architecture, Persian poetry, Persian paintings, behind which, little known in actuality, but having, like Greece in Europe, a vast prestige, is the art of China. This is what Akbar brings with him into India. But Akbar had Turkish, Mongol, and Persian blood in his veins. On his father's side he was seventh in descent from Timur (Tamerlane): through the mother of Babur he was descended from Jinghiz Khan.

The tremendous figures of these two world-conquerors dominated the historic scene of Asia. To us their conquests, wider than those of any conquerors before or since, seem almost meaningless: the tale of their fury, the obliterated cities, the smoke and flame, the shrieks and slaughter, is like the phantasmagoria of a frightful dream, followed by the absolute silence of the dead. Viewed from a like distance, would not the transient conquests of Napoleon, his 'sheep-worry of Europe'—it is Robert Bridges' apt and scornful phrase—appear much the same? But Jinghiz and Timur, for all their insane lust of destruction, were no savages (Timur, when he destroyed a city, always spared its artists); they were men of prodigious ability; their armies were controlled by iron discipline; their strategy and way of war continued to be Akbar's models. He could never wholly discard that military tradition, and retained some of its ferocious observances. And yet his conquests were different in kind. Having won Hindostan, he was resolved to become Indian, to belong wholly to that India which drew him on as if by some secret and unconscious affinity.

I do not suppose that Akbar had ever heard of Asoka, the greatest ruler of India in the past. Had he known of his aims and achievements, as they are now known through the labours of European scholars, we can conceive with what extreme interest he would have studied Asoka's career and his methods of administration. For Asoka's empire was even vaster than Akbar's: it embraced almost the whole of India, Nepal, and Kashmir.

Asoka was the grandson of Chandragupta, the Maurya king who had foiled the attempt of Seleucus, the satrap of Babylon, to renew and extend Alexander's temporary hold on Indian territory, and who had established a firm rule over Northern India. It was thus a settled empire to which Asoka succeeded: he had not to fight for security. There were, however, out-lying parts to be brought into the empire. And in the thirteenth year from his accession, prob-ably the year 261 B.C., Asoka conquered and annexed the kingdom of Kalinga, on the coast of the Bay of Bengal. This conquest was the turning-point of his whole life.

Caesar 'came, saw, and conquered.' Asoka conquered, and then saw. He saw what war and conquest meant. He saw that through him a hundred thousand of his fellow-beings had been killed, fifty thousand more had been taken into captivity, and myriads more had died or suffered violence. He was filled with remorse and sorrow. Thenceforth he began his new life. He resolved to be a conqueror; but the conquest was to be not of arms, but of the Sacred Law. This was a conquest 'full of joy,' and the emperor desired for all animated beings 'security, self-control, peace of mind, and joyousness.'

Asoka had adopted the Way of Buddha. Immediately after the Kalinga campaign, he became a lay disciple; and not long afterwards he became a Buddhist monk.

The conversion of Asoka was a momentous event in the history of mankind. Buddhism, till then a somewhat obscure sect, was set on its way to become a world-religion. Asoka reigned for about forty years, and never relaxed his missionary ardour. His edicts enjoining the duties of the Law on all his people were engraved on rocks far and wide through his dominions and on stone pillars wherever suitable stone existed. Nor was he content with preaching the Buddhist gospel to his own subjects; he sent missionaries to Syria, to Egypt, to Africa, Macedonia, Epirus.

Though a monk, Asoka led no life of sequestered contemplation. He was supremely active, and insisted on activity in others. 'Let small and great exert themselves,' he proclaimed.

'The welfare of the whole people' was his incessant concern. Not only did he preach the
duties of filial piety, of truth-telling, compas-
sion, almsgiving, the sanctity of all life, and
toleration for the genuine beliefs of others, but
the practical details of administration occupied
his thoughts. By the hot and dusty roads shady
trees bearing fruit were to be planted for the
comfort of both men and animals; wells were
to be dug, rest-houses built, watering-places
contrived, medicinal herbs were to be grown,
and hospitals founded for the sick.

Here was a ruler, unique among the great
rulers of mankind, who would assuredly have
engaged Akbar's sympathy and admiration,
though doubtless he would have found it hard
to contemplate the renunciation of war. Most
of all would he have been attracted by Asoka's
precept of toleration. Not because it was a
politic toleration, like the Roman toleration,
springing from indifference, but because, like
Akbar's own attitude of mind, it sprang from
respect for sincere faith, of whatever professed
denomination. It is true that he had no such
thorny problems to deal with as confronted the
great Mogul. The various faiths of India had
much in common: there were no such militant
claims as those of Islam and Christianity.

Moreover, it was in a sense easy for him to renounce war just because his empire was the inheritance of successful war.

Standing in the full daylight of history, Akbar appears to us between two shadowy yet strangely contrasted worlds: between the world of his Central Asian ancestors, a world of torrential human energy, idolising that energy for its own sake, and possessed with the fever of the hunt, whether of beasts or of men—for Akbar's gigantic hunts are like an echo of Tamerlane's campaigns of slaughter—between that world of furious action, passing like a dream, and the world of India, which could revel indeed in luxuries and cruelties, but which could also produce the exalted spirits of Buddha and Asoka, speaking to us from a far remoter past than those wild conquerors, but with voices that still live and move us. Akbar, too, is possessed with insatiable energy, he seems action incarnate; and yet at the core of his nature is something alien to all that, something that craves for thought and contemplation, that seeks justice and desires gentleness.

III

BUT what of his more immediate ancestry?

Once, returning from a campaign, Akbar questioned Monserrate about Sebastian, king of Portugal, who had fallen fighting against the Moors in 1578. When he had heard the story, he burst out, 'I can never sufficiently praise the heroism of those who fight hand to hand and in deadly earnest. But I shall never cease to condemn the cowardice of those who prefer the safety of their bodies to the eternal glory of War!'

The joy of danger, the eternal glory of war! It might be the voice of Babur. From the June day when his father—short, stout, careless, hasty —visiting his pigeons in a pigeon-house on the top of a precipice was suddenly hurled to the bottom, pigeons and all, by a landslip and transferred to another world, Babur, then a boy of eleven, had to fight for his crown or his life or his ambition; and he loved it. The moment that he heard that his father was dead he sprang on horseback. Three invasions menaced his capital. He had to meet and quell them all.

Three years later, he seized Samarcand, the city of his forefather Timur, the city of his dreams. After a hundred days of possession, he lost it. Twice later he was to hold it for a brief time: then he lost it for ever. His Usbeg enemies were too strong for him. And he had lost his little kingdom of Ferghana too. His great ambition had been to sit on Timur's throne in Samarcand. He renounced that cherished dream, but a throne he was determined to have, while he tramped the hills an exile among the shepherds. He had undying confidence in his star. His thoughts turned southward. Kabul was in a state of anarchy, following the death of its king, who was Babur's uncle. He decided to march on Kabul. He took it and became king. At Kabul he was on the road to India: and according to his own account, the thought of subduing Hindostan was already in his mind as soon as he had become master of Kabul. Long before, a very old woman had told him tales of Timur's invasion of India: and he had never forgotten. If he could not have Timur's throne in Samarcand, he might follow in his ancestor's footsteps southward. But it was twenty-two years after the conquest of Kabul before he entered Delhi in triumph and founded the empire that Akbar was to rule.

In temperament and in certain outstanding traits of character Akbar resembled his grandfather. But we shall note the differences.

Babur in his perfectly frank and delightful *Memoirs,* one of the most remarkable books of its kind ever written, gives us a vivid self-portrait. He has the Mongol restlessness in his blood: but he is much more a Turk, and has no words strong enough for his hatred and contempt of the Mongols he knew. With enormous energy and absolutely fearless courage, he is rapid in his decisions, often succeeding by his swift action but often betrayed into disaster by his reckless confidence. But he could profit by experience. He trained his army to a high pitch of efficiency: he became a master of the art of war. Severe in discipline, he could at times be savagely cruel (the Mongol strain perhaps coming out), yet in general he was chivalrous, loyal, generous, and forgiving. He hated falseness above all things.

Babur might appear to be nothing more than a splendid adventurer of exceptional ability, but that he seems, all through the amazing vicissitudes of his career, to have nourished the dream of founding an empire, and to have succeeded, not by the mere luck of a soldier of fortune but by a singular pertinacity and belief in his destiny. And even as an adventurer he is remarkable. This hardy soldier, this marvellous fighter, who swims every river he comes across, astonishes us by his singular sensibility. A man could win his heart by his love of poetry as surely as by his swordsmanship. Was he flying from his enemies in bitter weather with a handful of followers? He would compose a few couplets as he rode, and his spirits revived as by magic. But it was his intense delight in the beauty of the world which made so large a part of his unquenchable zest in life. Was ever such a lover of flowers? His first thought in a newly acquired territory was to make a garden, himself superintending the disposition of the beds and the leading of fresh runnels of water among them. In the year before his death in 1530, amid the heat and dust of India, he writes: 'The other day they brought me a musk-melon: as I cut it up I felt a deep homesickness and sense of exile from my native land, and I could not help weeping.'

For Babur never felt at home in the plains of India. He pined for his native hills: for Ferghana, that delectable province set among the mountains in the midst of Asia, with its cool air, its leaping brooks, its fertile fields, its grapes and melons and pomegranates. Ferghana was a favoured land: was it not the marvellous horses of Ferghana which were coveted from afar by the emperors of China? Kabul, with its mountain climate, though less adorable than Ferghana, was congenial to Babur's nature. India he found ugly and unattractive. It is true he meant to stay there, not merely to invade and plunder as other raiders from the North had done before him, but he meant to rule as a foreign conqueror over the Indians. His policy did not go beyond the policy of Timur: it was that of giving his lieutenants the government of apportioned districts: and an empire founded on these lines was bound to dissolve among the quarrels and ambitions of these deputy-rulers, as the vast empire of Timur had dissolved so swiftly. That it did not crumble away, that it endured till the nineteenth century, is due solely to Akbar's larger policy and constructive foresight. It is the measure of Akbar's greatness. To a temperament akin to that of his grandfather, there was added in Akbar a more masculine intellect. Babur's poetry and sensibility to beauty become in him a voracious curiosity and an ardent interest in religious problems. Where Babur was romantic, Akbar was a realist.

The story of Babur's death is a fit close to

his romantic career. His son Humayun was dangerously ill, and his life was despaired of. Babur vowed he would give his life for his son's. He prayed earnestly, pacing round his son's sick-bed, that his vow might be accepted: and it was so. Humayun recovered; Babur died.

Humayun recovered, to find himself emperor. But though Hindostan had been conquered, it needed a strong hand to hold it: and Humayun had not the strength required. He was now a young man of twenty-two. With his narrow shoulders, slight stoop, long face and pointed beard, he had an aspect of fragility. He was addicted to opium. Though not a weakling, there was a childish side to his character. He was naturally inclined to be more interested in the different colours of his dresses than in state-craft and command. But he was forced into action. He was obliged to make over the government of the Punjab and Afghanistan to his brother Kamran. Even the throne of Delhi must be fought for. The governor of Bihar, Sher Shah, a very able ruler, saw his opportunity and attacked. Humayun was disastrously defeated, and fled with a few followers into the deserts of Sind.

IV

One morning, late in November 1542, Humayun, encamped on the shores of a small lake with a force of some two thousand horsemen lent him by a friendly chief, saw the dust of a group of riders approaching at speed over the desert. The homeless emperor had need to be wary. For two years, driven from his kingdom by the victories of Sher Shah, he had been wandering in the sandy wilderness of Sind, to the west of India, with a handful of followers. He could settle on no plan. He knew not whom he could trust. His own brothers, Kamran and Askari, were his rivals: doubtful friends, probable enemies. Swift riders were only too likely to be bearers of bad news. But on this day Humayun could hope. The riders came from the direction of Umarkot, a little fortified town some twenty miles distant from his camp: and at Umarkot he had left his young wife expecting shortly to be a mother.

The messenger rode into the camp with joyful signs. Hamida had been delivered of a boy. Humayun had an heir. Here at last was something of good augury: and Humayun rejoiced in the thought of his beloved girl-wife (she was only fifteen when she gave birth to her first-born). She had not been over-willing to marry a fugitive king without a crown; but she had charmed his heart, he had wooed her with ardour, and now she had given him an heir and hope.

Such an occasion should have been celebrated with pomp and ceremony and the giving of many presents. What was the proud father to do in his poverty? His servant Jauhar, who was there, has recorded the scene: how Jauhar was ordered to bring a bag of silver coins and a silver bracelet and a pod of musk; and how Humayun ordered the silver to be given back to the owners from whom it had been taken (a convenient mode of largesse), and taking the pod of musk broke it on a porcelain dish and distributed it among the chief of his followers, and said, 'This is all the present I can afford to make you on the birth of my son, whose fame will, I trust, be one day expanded over all the world, as the perfume of the musk now fills this tent.' The child was given the name of Akbar. He was born on the twenty-third day of November 1542.

But Humayun could not at once have the joy

of embracing wife and son. He was on the
march, and did not rest till he had taken possession of the town of Jun and made his en-
campment secure against surprise. At last, on
28th December, Hamida and her baby arrived,
and Humayun for the first time set eyes on his
son. Till July of the following year he stayed
at Jun, planning what he should do next. The
birth of his son strengthened, no doubt, the
resolution, which he had never given up, to
recover by some means or other his lost kingdom. For though he had many weaknesses, and
was no master of war like his father, he had a
certain tenacity of purpose even in circumstances the most desperate. He could not for
ever roam the deserts of Sind. Should he try
for Kandahar? Once there, he might get help
from the Persian Shah. It was on Kandahar
that he decided to march. But there were his
two brothers, Kamran and Askari, to be reckoned with. Kamran was ruler of Kabul, and
Askari, the younger brother, held the province
of Kandahar under Kamran. Their attitude
was doubtful: but the hazard must be run.
Humayun had a long and difficult march before
him. He had to cross the Indus and then find a
way over the mountain-barriers of Baluchistan.
Arrived at the frontier of Kandahar province,

Humayun received sudden and dismaying news.
Askari, his brother, was in motion to attack him
with a force far outnumbering his own. There
was nothing for it but to flee, and not a moment
to be lost. There was a hurried consultation.
The child Akbar had been brought so far in his
mother's arms: but in the mountains of Afghanistan the extremes of heat and cold would be
fatal to a one-year-old baby, now that they must
travel on horseback and at forced speed. The
child was left behind in the care of Jauhar.
They were even short of horses, and Hamida
must ride on Humayun's horse with him. The
fugitives dashed away to the mountains, and
were hardly gone when Askari swooped down
on the camp and captured his infant nephew.

If Askari was tempted to forestall fortune and
(after a favourite practice of ambitious members of Asian royal houses) to 'make sure' by
getting rid of a future rival, he resisted the
temptation: or it may be that he was taken by
the sturdy child. He carried it off to Kandahar, the faithful Jauhar in attendance; and
there it was treated well.

Meanwhile, Humayun and his girl-wife and
forty men continued their desperate course.
Humayun had now resolved to flee to Persia and
seek assistance from the Shah. Having received

friendly messages in answer to his overtures, he
made the long journey over Persia to Kazvin,
where Shah Tahmasp then held his court, in
the far north-west. Shah Tahmasp received
Humayun cordially. But he soon tired of playing host to a fugitive who gave no signs of going.
For about a year Humayun lingered at the
Persian court. This sojourn in a luxurious
and cultured centre, after years of precarious
wanderings and hardships in desert plains and
mountains, made a deep impression on the
Mogul prince, just as Babur before him had
been impressed with the brilliant culture of
Herat when Persian art was producing its finest
masterpieces. He was naturally fond of books
and learning, and a lover of art: and at Kazvin
he saw what he hoped one day to have round
him at Delhi—a gathering of poets, wits,
scholars, and artists. What is called the Mogul
School of Indian painting, so ardently fostered
by Akbar when he came to the throne, had its
origin in Humayun's visit to Persia. Shah
Tahmasp, though not a very estimable monarch, was a great patron of the arts, and some
of the most famous painters of Persia were
working at Tabriz.

Late in 1544, Humayun was dismissed with
a promise of Persian troops to help him win

back his patrimony. Before a year was over Kandahar had surrendered, and Askari was pardoned by his brother. Humayun advanced on Kabul. His other brother, Kamran, abandoned the city, and Humayun established himself in his place. The little Akbar was already at Kabul; his mother, left behind at Kandahar, was sent for, and the three were united once more. Not that their troubles were over; for Humayun's position was still insecure, and Kamran alternated insincere submissions and reconciliations with open and ferocious hostility or secret intrigues. But Humayun during the nine years of his stay at Kabul had time to gather his forces for the long-cherished attempt to recover India, and to educate the son who was to inherit his recovered throne.

To educate? But it was one thing to provide instructors, and another to persuade the pupil to learn. And never was a boy more refractory. Four tutors in turn did their utmost: the boy refused even to learn his letters. Humayun, with his scholarly tastes, was annoyed; he reproved his much-loved son for his idleness, and gave him fond and fatherly advice. It was of little avail. Akbar was a cheerful and accomplished truant. From the very day of his birth he had been in the midst of danger, ad-

venture, and desperate enterprise; he was
enamoured of outdoor life, and threw his whole
heart into masculine sports and exercises. He
liked being with animals—horses, dogs, and
camels—and became expert in pigeon-flying, a
sport of which he remained excessively fond.
In riding, polo, and swordplay he was highly
trained as well as efficient by nature. He became an excellent shot. And his reluctance to
learn to read was not combined with that aver-
sion from things of the mind so often found in
the English schoolboy devoted to games. On
the contrary, he delighted in being read to by
others, and, with his amazing memory, soon
had by heart whole poems of the Persian poets,
especially those of the Sufi mystics.

Humayun would also have his son taught
something of the art of painting. In 1550 he
invited to Kabul two young Persian artists of
great distinction, Mir Sayyid Ali and Abdus
Samad, and these two became his principal
court painters, and afterwards went to Delhi.
Both Humayun and the boy Akbar took lessons in the Persian style of drawing. In the
Gulistan Library at Teheran there is a minia-
ture by Abdus Samad, in which we see the
little prince among his craftsmen, and in an-

other part of the picture he presents a drawing commemorating the scene to the emperor. At this time, too, Humayun, possessed as ever by the dream of recovering his throne and by his pride of ancestry, had himself painted with the Timurid princes, and Timur himself, around him. The Persian artist produced a dazzling picture. The setting was among the hills in spring, with pomegranates in flower by an iris-bordered stream, and a rustling plane tree overhead against a golden sky. Slim red pillars supported a pavilion in which sat Humayun facing his terrible ancestor Timur, and in a semi-circle below sat the descendants of Timur who were Humayun's ancestors. At a later date the figure of Timur was effaced, and portraits of Akbar, with his son and grandson, substituted by an Indian painter. The picture is now in the British Museum.

So in peaceful pursuits, variegated by frequent alarms and excursions, these years at Kabul passed, until the favourable moment came when the long-planned descent on India might be carried out with good hope of success.

In November 1554 Humayun started. Akbar was now twelve years old. After crossing the Indus father and son had a solemn audience together, and the blessing of Heaven was invoked on their enterprise. There was a new ruler on the throne of Delhi, a far weaker man than his predecessor Salim Shah Sur, who had died this year. Hindostan too was in a disunited and chaotic state, disaffected to the Afghan rulers. The time therefore was propitious. And Humayun, no great captain himself, relied on a young man, Bairam Khan, an able soldier of high character, who was put in command of the army.

The campaign was successful. Early in 1555 Humayun occupied Lahore, and in June a great victory, with which the young Akbar was officially credited, gained him Delhi. The lost throne was at last recovered.

But not for long was it to be enjoyed. Akbar was sent in charge of Bairam Khan, now appointed his guardian, to the Punjab, while Humayun remained in the capital. Much was to be done if the Moguls were to make their hold secure. Humayun planned to garrison the chief cities with his troops, and was busy with the task of organisation when, on a Friday evening in January 1556, as the sunset call to prayers was heard, he tripped and fell down the steep steps leading from the roof of a tower, used as a library, and broke his skull.[1] Three days later he was dead.

Akbar received the news of his father's death at Kalanaur, and in a garden at that place was formally enthroned, on a throne which still exists.

[1] Mr. Payne, the editor of Du Jarric, suggests that possibly Humayun was an epileptic and that a fit caused his fall.

V

So, like his grandfather before him, Akbar gained a crown while still a boy, but a crown for which he had to fight. There were rival claimants. One was Sikandar Sur, a nephew of that able ruler Sher Shah, and it was against him that Bairam Khan and Akbar had been sent to the Punjab. But a more formidable opponent appeared in a certain Hindu named Hemu, who took the field for his master, Muhammad Shah Adil, lately in occupation of Delhi, where he had usurped the throne but had soon been driven out. Hemu was a capable general. He defeated the Mogul forces and took Delhi and Agra, and puffed up by his victory, assumed sovereignty on his own account. It was a critical situation. But Hemu had to reckon with Bairam Khan, who would listen to no counsels of retreat to Kabul, and advancing with Akbar met the enemy's vastly superior army, with its huge array of elephants, on the field of Panipat, where Babur had won the throne of Delhi. An arrow pierced Hemu through the eye, and his troops scattered in dismay. Hemu was captured, and Bairam Khan bade Akbar despatch the wretched prisoner, but the boy shrank from using his sword on a wounded and helpless man. Delhi and Agra were retaken. Sikandar Sur was pursued, and after a long resistance surrendered in 1557. He was generously treated. By that time the other claimants to the throne had died or disappeared from the scene. Akbar was free to rule, and to organise his realm.

During these first years of his reign Akbar's education was continued. But while he delighted in the training of his body, and in all skilful exercises, he still refused to read, and preferred to acquire knowledge of books by ear. At this time he appeared to those around him as a healthy, athletic boy, enjoying life to the full, passionately fond of hunting and games, and paying little attention to politics, finance, and the business of state. There is a portrait of him made about this time. Seen in profile, with smooth cheeks and lips and long curling hair, an animated expression in his eyes, and wearing a purple coat, he stands smelling a flower which he holds to his nostrils. Before him is blue sky and empty plain. Pose and presentment belong to current convention, but

41

here seem specially happy in the portrait of eager youth with all the world before it.

Yet, according to Abul Fazl, though he appeared indifferent to affairs, his mind was busy; he was shrewdly taking stock of his supporters and testing their loyalty in the atmosphere of intrigue and counter-intrigue which pervaded the court. And perhaps an intimate observer might also have detected symptoms of something different and singular, of strange capacities for melancholy, beneath the outward glow of restless activity. Even at the age of fourteen Akbar could feel a sudden overwhelming dissatisfaction with the world. On a day in 1557 such a mood fell upon him. He felt the presence of 'short-sighted men,' whose thoughts were all of this world, unendurable. He appeared to be full of anger and impatience, and sent for a certain horse of Iraqi breed, noted for its high mettle and vicious temper, a horse he often chose to ride. He would have none attend him, not even a groom; and mounting, he rode away into the desert plain—he was then at Agra—consumed with a passion to be away from men and utterly alone.

Out of sight and in solitude, he dismounted and 'communed with God.' The fiery horse at once galloped off and disappeared in the distance. Akbar remained alone on the plain, immersed in his ecstasy. But after a time, his heart refreshed and eased, he came to himself and looked around. He was in absolute solitude, and surrounded by silence. There was no one to attend him, no horse to carry him home. For a time he stood perplexed: then suddenly he saw the horse Hairan galloping out of the distance towards him. It came up and stood still beside him. The young king, astonished, mounted him, and rode back to his camp. It seemed to him a mysterious and divine intimation that he must return to his fellows and resume his work in the world.

A strange experience for a boy of fourteen. But Akbar was already steeped in the mysticism of the Persian poets, whose verses he had learnt by heart at Kabul: this mysticism appealed to his cast of mind: and, as we shall see, this adventure was the prelude to other experiences of a like nature.

He was soon plunged in the delights of sport, this time with elephants. At Kabul he had dogs, horses, and camels; but now India gave him something new to master. An animal so huge and powerful, so swift in movement for all its bulk and weight, so intelligent, delighted Akbar. And if it was fierce, vicious, and murderous, so much the more worthy to be tamed and made submissive to his will. When a certain elephant had killed its driver and savaged other men and had become a terror to all, Akbar, 'as he was walking between the garden and the courtyard,' placed his foot on the elephant's tusk, smilingly took his seat, and set the great beast to fight with another quarrelsome elephant. In the middle of the fight, when he saw that the driver of the other elephant had lost control, he leapt from his own elephant to the other. This and other feats of skill, courage, and agility are recorded by Abul Fazl; and the emperor Jahangir in his memoirs confirms his witness by later instances of his father's power to subdue the wildest and most unruly elephant to his will. Akbar's prowess caused astonishment and admiration, but also solicitude; and on one of these occasions Bairam Khan came to prostrate himself at the throne in gratitude to God for the preservation of his young sovereign's life. He distributed largesses also, to avert the evil eye.

Bairam Khan belonged to the Shia sect, the orthodox sect in Persia; on this account he was disliked by the Sunnis, the dominant sect in India. But he raised more active enmity through his position as Protector. There were others who coveted his power and wished to get the young emperor under their own influence. Moreover, he was still a young man, and might well be suspected of cherishing ambitions on his own account. Perhaps he was not altogether free from such ambitions. Those who were to be his most formidable enemies were the ladies of the court, who after the defeat of Hemu had been escorted from Kabul to India. The queen-mother, Hamida, was then thirty years of age, and, now that after all the vicissitudes of her life success and empire were assured to her son, she was not unwilling to taste the new delights of power. With her came, among other ladies, Maham Anaga, chief of Akbar's nurses, who brought her son, Adham Khan. Maham Anaga was a woman of little scruple and great ambition.

It was Bairam Khan who had won back the crown for Humayun. Without his skill and captaincy Akbar could hardly have retained it. Akbar was no ingrate by nature, but, conscious of his own abilities, he chafed at the restrictions imposed on him, especially as he was kept short of money. During the next three years these feelings increased, and were assiduously encouraged by the ladies of the court, and by all those whom Bairam had offended. A Pro-

tector, apt to think himself indispensable, a
strong man presuming on his strength; and a
youthful emperor, also a strong nature and
eager to enter on his full inheritance—it was
inevitable that a clash should come between
them. The intrigues of the court went on;
secret accusations against Bairam were continually being made. In 1560 matters came to a
head. Akbar was now in his eighteenth year.

Maham Anaga, the chief nurse, took the lead
in the conspiracy, and instigated Akbar to write
a letter to Bairam Khan, announcing that he
had determined to take the reins of government
into his own hands and instructing Bairam to
make the pilgrimage to Mecca, 'upon which
you have been so long intent.' Thus was
Bairam disgraced. Worse than this, a disloyal
servant of his own was chosen to follow him
with an armed force and 'pack him off to
Mecca.' At this Bairam was stung into rebellion. He was defeated and brought a prisoner
to Akbar, who forgave him. He was given
ample means to proceed to Mecca in such state
as fitted his rank and eminence, and started off
to the coast. But his pilgrimage was never fulfilled. At Patan he was attacked by a party
of Afghans and stabbed to death. His four-
year-old son, Abdurrahim, was brought to court

and grew up under Akbar's protection to become the greatest of his nobles. We can divine from this a feeling of remorse on Akbar's part for the shabby treatment accorded to his father, to whom Akbar owed so much. Bairam Khan was brave and loyal: his high ability unquestioned. He may have shown himself arrogant, but he had fallen a victim to the intrigues of smaller men and of jealous women.

Maham Anaga enjoyed her triumph; Akbar for the time being seems to have been entirely under her influence. But before long she was to overreach herself, through her ambitions for her son.

VI

MEANWHILE, the young emperor was called to active efforts in the field. The surrender of Gwalior and the annexation of Jaunpur had strengthened Akbar's frontiers: he was now determined to undertake the conquest of Malwa, a kingdom ruled over by a lover of wine and song and music, Baz Bahadur; and Maham Anaga's son, Adham Khan, was put in command of the expedition. Baz Bahadur's favourite wife, Rupmati, was famous for her charm and beauty. Their loves have been celebrated in song, and are the theme of many an Indian painting. We see them riding together among the hills by moonlight, or resting by the mountain streams. Before the battle which decided his fate, Baz Bahadur had given commands, according to Indian custom, that in the event of his defeat the lovely Rupmati should be killed with his other wives and concubines, so that they should not fall into his enemies' hands. He was defeated. Just as the victorious troops entered, Rupmati was stabbed but still lived. Adham Khan sent to search for her, and tried to take her for his own, but she poisoned herself to escape him. Adham Khan also kept back the women and the spoils he had captured, instead of sending them to court, and massacred the defeated population with a bloodthirsty delight.

Akbar was angered, and took swift measures. Leaving Agra in haste, he surprised the delinquent general, who behaved 'like a bewildered moth' and humbly prostrated himself. His mother, Maham Anaga, hurried after Akbar to smooth matters over, and succeeded for the moment. She scolded her son and forced him to make reparation. But Adham Khan was incorrigible. He bribed his mother's servants to let him steal two special beauties from the harem of Baz Bahadur who had passed into Akbar's harem, thinking that in the bustle of departure it would not be noticed. But he was found out, and the women were sent for by Akbar. Maham, afraid that if they came before the emperor her son's treachery would be disclosed, had them both put secretly to death. It speaks much for this woman's extraordinary plausibility and her ascendancy over Akbar that he condoned this cruel murder, though perhaps he never forgot it.

On the way home a tigress with five cubs

came out of the jungle in the path of the royal cavalcade. Akbar at once encountered it alone, and while his escort turned pale and sweated with apprehension, killed it with a single blow of his sword.

At this time Akbar began a habit of disguising himself from time to time and mixing with his subjects in order to hear their opinion of things. On one such occasion, when there was a great assemblage of pilgrims and others near Agra, he went among the crowd by night 'contemplating humanity,' and was recognised by a vagabond. Instantly distorting his features and squinting with his eyes, he completely changed his appearance: the vagabond's surmise was discredited, and the emperor quietly stole away.

These nocturnal adventures were in keeping with Akbar's boundless curiosity. But it was something more than curiosity. Surrounded by flatterers and intriguers, he could not expect to know the truth unless he sought it out for himself. He was not yet twenty; but he meant to rule, and in order to rule wisely, he must understand the condition of the people. In spite of his outward devotion to sport and hunting, it is clear that he was thinking deeply and paid far more attention to state affairs than he let his courtiers know.

Maham Anaga still regarded herself as virtual prime minister. But in 1561 she and her party received a severe check.

Shams ud-Din Khan arrived from Kabul and was given control of political, financial, and military affairs. Maham was superseded. At the same time her brutal son, Adham Khan, was recalled from the government of Malwa. Apparently Akbar wished to reform him and to have him under his eye. But he had not been long in Agra when he surpassed, in a supreme outrage, all his former audacities. On a day in May 1561 Akbar was asleep in his harem, adjoining the hall where the new prime minister, Shams ud-Din, was engaged in public business with other officials. To them strode in Adham Khan with a gang behind him: heedless of their courtesies, he advanced with loud and insolent threats. Then he signed to two of his followers: they set upon Shams ud-Din with their swords: he ran out, was again struck, and fell dead. The noise roused Akbar. Already Adham Khan was at Akbar's door, bent on a greater murder; but the door was bolted and guarded. Akbar had been told of what had happened, and went out by another way. He saw the blood-stained corpse.

The two met on the terrace. Adham Khan

tried to seize the emperor's sword, but Akbar felled him with his fist. Then, terrible in his rage, he ordered his men to bind and take up the senseless miscreant and throw him from the terrace. But the men were timid, and fear made them half-hearted in the business. Adham Khan was found below, still breathing. He was carried up and again flung headlong; his neck was broken and his brains scattered.

Akbar retired to his harem. Maham Anaga, hearing that her son had committed an outrage and had been imprisoned, rose terrified from a sick-bed and came in supplication to the emperor. Akbar spoke briefly: 'Adham Khan killed our minister; we have punished him.' The wretched woman still did not know that her son was dead. She could only murmur, 'You did well.' A little after she learnt the truth. 'How was he killed?' she asked. 'We don't know,' they answered, 'but there is the mark of a mace on his face.' The mace was Akbar's fist. Maham did not dare to complain openly, but 'inwardly she was wounded by a thousand deadly blows.' She shut herself up and wept; her illness grew worse, and in six weeks she was dead. Akbar was free at last to govern in reality.

VII

Thus it was that Akbar emerged from 'behind
the veil' (in Abul Fazl's phrase), and now
openly and in person undertook the supervision
of his government. The corruption and em-
bezzlement which had flourished under Maham
Anaga and her faction were stopped, though
the chiefs who had shared in her intrigues and
connived at the treachery of her son were
treated with singular generosity. It was now
that the old practice of Muslim invaders of en-
slaving Indian prisoners of war was abolished
by edict.

Already, earlier in the year 1562, Akbar had
married a Rajput princess of Jaipur, who was
to become the mother of his successor Jahangir.
Such a marriage was a symbol of his irrevocable
union with India and her destinies. He was no
more the foreign invader, but India's adopted
son. The subtle influences of this Hindu marriage were fruitful of consequences.

About this time, too, the most famous of Indian singers and musicians, Tansen of Gwalior,
was summoned to court. He was received with

great honour and with lavish gifts. Akbar loved music, and studied it to some purpose: Tansen became a special favourite.

Another Hindu singer and musician, Birbal, was to become one of Akbar's intimates and dearest friends, and he loved to listen to his jokes and stories.

Yet Akbar's inner nature had undergone a shock. He had always been devoted to his nurse, Maham Anaga; he had overlooked the faults of her worthless son, and given him far more chances than he deserved: yet this man had treacherously tried to murder him, and who could tell how far his own mother was innocent? He had trusted one man after another who had betrayed his trust. He realised that he must rely on himself alone: but what a vast burden he was called upon to shoulder! Where was the truth? How would God reveal it to him? He mixed in disguise with the commonest of his subjects. He broke off from hunting to consort with any dust-stained hermit or fakir, who might prove a physician of the soul. He questioned the learned, and, though he forbore to deride them, he found their answers profitless and empty. Now on completing his twentieth year, in spite of all his achievements and his intense zest in life, he 'experienced an eternal bitterness.' 'From the lack of spiritual provision for my last journey my soul was seized with exceeding sorrow.'

The mystical illumination which had come to the boy of fourteen, when he rode away from men to be in utter solitude, had been an experience isolated from the rest of his ardent and manifold activities. Yet it showed what was in the depths of his nature. He had an unquenchable thirst for truth, for spiritual reality. Hypocrisy and pretension imposed on him not at all. He desired an anchor for his soul. He desired to know the Divine Will, and to act in accordance with it. But how was the Divine Will to be known? This was Akbar's restless search for all the days that he lived. What wonder if, bearing alone the burden of an empire and answerable for the welfare of millions, he experienced fits of deep dejection?

Even his reckless feats of daring which filled his courtiers with consternation—as when, mounted on the fiercest and wickedest of elephants, he made him fight with another elephant till his own victoriously chased the other across the Jumna, half-submerging the bridge of boats in their wild rush—even these, if we may believe his own explanation, were inspired not merely by physical exultation in his own strength and skill, but by a deeper prompting. Was it the Divine Will that he should die? Had he offended God and gone contrary to His commands? Then it were better not to go on living. He would put it to the proof. For if God intended he should die, by taking such fearful odds he offered himself for death. But if by a wonder he should be preserved, it was a sign that he should live.

These spiritual wrestlings with himself were hidden from the world. Men saw that their young king was indeed a man. More than his extraordinary physical prowess, his bold resolution and swift action impressed all those around him; and far and wide his manifest determination to treat Hindu and Muslim with equal justice won him loyal adherents where he might have had obstinate enemies.

Further measures of wise generosity still more conciliated the Hindus. In 1563 Akbar was in camp at Mathura, hunting tigers. Mathura is a holy place, the resort of pilgrims.

And now he learnt that the government had made a practice of levying a tax on all pilgrims to the holy places of India, bringing in a revenue of some millions of rupees. He was indignant. The Hindus might be wrong in their modes of worship, but the pilgrims assembled to worship God; it was surely not God's pleasure that they should be taxed. Forthwith the tax was remitted throughout the empire. Exhilarated by this merciful act, the young emperor started to walk the thirty-six miles from Mathura to Agra in a day. Of all his followers, only an exhausted three arrived with him at Agra. He outstripped his court in body: how much more in mind!

Early in the next year, still in the same mood of generous impulse, he resolved to remit the poll-tax levied on all adult males who were not Muslims. Here again was a heavy sacrifice of revenue. It was an assertion of Akbar's will and conscience against a tradition of all the Muslim conquerors of India, sanctioned by centuries of custom, against all his advisers, against the desire of his mother and his family. In a young man of twenty-two these acts astonished.

The power of custom to control and limit our actions is immense: more incalculable still is its power to blind us. Every age is astonished at the iniquities and cruelties that its predecessors, with no consciousness of wrong, authorised or acquiesced in. As it was with our grandfathers, so it will be with us, because of the things we have permitted in our world.

We have seen the young Akbar tormented
inwardly by doubts about himself, seized with
sudden and overwhelming sorrow, seeking to
know the Divine Will. We have seen him
penetrated with a sense of the universal in humanity, and rising up against armed custom and
overthrowing it, in defiance of all his elders and
their counsel.

But now we are to see him under a different
light, showing another facet of his many-sided
nature. The restless blood, the fierce vitality
of his ancestry, were a power within him that
could not be quelled. In so far as he was a
thinking being, he was wise, tolerant, generous,
capable of seeing far beyond his own time and
carrying his thoughts into bold execution; but
he was a born man of action; and immersed in
action, heated with his own furious energy, he
was capable of savage things. Firm on his
throne and dependent on no counsellor, he now
began the career of conquest and annexation
which was only to end with his death. It would
never, I imagine, have entered into his head
that such a career was inconsistent with his
spiritual aspirations. He knew that he was a
ruler of men; he believed, and with reason,
that his rule was beneficent; doubtless he believed that God had destined him to bring

India, with whose destiny he had resolved to identify himself more and more, under his beneficent sway. After all, it was by right of conquest only that he held his throne; and it was not for nothing that the blood of Timur flowed in his veins. Without scruple, therefore, he attacked neighbouring states without provocation and annexed them to his dominions. Here ancestral custom was unquestioned.

Akbar's mind was restless as his body. He was intensely interested in discussion and speculation on religious matters: but in the region of thought he was tentative, hesitating, uncertain: it was a taste, a passionate preoccupation, that he showed, but not an inborn genius. In action, on the other hand, it was genius that shone forth. As a born painter is absorbed in painting, as a musician in music, so Akbar became absorbed in the intoxicating delight of action. Here his touch was certain, his instinct swift. And for men born with the genius and zest for action strong and irrepressible within them, there are few outlets that do not bring them into conflict with their fellowmen; they can scarce escape the desire to subdue and conquer in one way or another. What we are to note in Akbar is this: that having satisfied his instinctive will to conquer, he returns to his other self, he becomes humane and generous. The peoples whom he conquered accepted his rule and were reconciled to subjection. As with Caesar's conquest of Gaul, ruthless in bloodshed as it was, the final consequence was beneficent for after-generations: though our sympathies may be more with Vercingetorix than with Caesar, and more with Durgavati than with Akbar.

Durgavati was regent and virtual queen of the country of the Gonds. She was a woman of heroic mould: had fought many battles and won them all. She hunted tigers and was an unerring shot. But more than this, she was a just and capable administrator, beloved of all her people. Asaf Khan was the general sent by Akbar to subdue her kingdom. And he succeeded. Durgavati was driven back: her soldiers began to desert her: and in the last of her brave fights, wounded with two arrows, she chose to die by her own hand rather than become a captive. Immense treasure was taken, most of which Asaf Khan kept for himself.

It is one of the recorded 'Happy Sayings' of Akbar, that 'a monarch should be ever intent on conquest, otherwise his enemies rise in arms against him.' Excuses for war and conquest are easily invented by their promoters; but though in this case Akbar's aim was merely to extend his dominions, his contention had more justification than most such pretexts. For it is certain that had he sat still at Agra, content with what he had won already, he would have been continually embroiled in wars of defence. He was always having to deal with rebellions in one direction or another: there were always other claimants to his throne. Even as late as 1581 it was only by swift measures that he saved his kingdom.

Whether he was led on, step by step—'appetite growing with eating'—or whether from the first he had determined on a grand, far-reaching scheme of annexation, to include, if possible, all India, we cannot tell. But in the result it was the same thing.

Like a thorn in the consciousness of Akbar was the great Rajput stronghold of Chitor. He meant to have all Upper India under his way: but the Rajput chieftains, with very few exceptions, proudly held aloof from him, or defied him from their mountains and their fortified castles.

In 1567 Akbar decided to attack, and in October began the siege of Chitor. A great mass of rock, eight miles in circumference, rises abruptly from the plain. All round the heights ran fortifications enclosing the town, with many fine buildings and monuments. There was an abundant supply of water. The Rajputs of Mewar were famous for their chivalry and martial virtues. Fate was truly unkind when, just at the moment of greatest menace to their independence, the reigning rana, Udai Singh, happened to be a man not only quite unequal in ability to resist the Mogul arms and Akbar's generalship, but a coward unworthy of the Rajput name. At the rumour of Akbar's approach he fled from Chitor and hid himself in a distant refuge. A chief called Jaimall Rathor assumed command of the defence. Methodically and carefully Akbar invested the hill-fortress. Long trains of oxen struggled up steep paths dragging the siege-guns into position. Direct assaults were made, but were repulsed again and again. In December two mines were exploded, but were badly timed, so that the storming party which rushed into the breach made by the first were blown to pieces by the second. The breach was mended: the fort held out. A covered way had been begun to protect the besiegers as they advanced; this was gradually completed.

On 23rd February Akbar, from a loophole

in the covered way, noticed a conspicuous figure
on the breach giving orders and directing the
defenders. He took a good aim with his mus-
ket, fired, and the man fell. Soon afterwards
the besiegers could see great flames arising from
certain places in the city, and looked at each
other, not knowing what this might mean.
Then Bhagwan Das, the Rajput prince now
allied to Akbar by marriage and serving with
the Mogul army, said, 'It is the *jauhar,*' that
is, the terrible ceremony of burning the women
of a rajah slain in battle, that the honour of his
household might be protected. By this they
knew that Akbar's shot had killed Jaimall
Rathor, the commander of the fortress. This
was the end: for the death of the commander
in Indian battles means defeat for his soldiers.
In vain the Rajput warriors rushed to die for
Chitor, and Rajput women, old and of tender
years, joined their ranks and fought by their
sides. At dawn on the morning after, Akbar,
mounted on an elephant, entered the fallen
fortress; but even then there was desperate resistance. Eight thousand Rajputs, it is said,
fighting to the last for the honour of their race,
perished in the final storming of the city.
Akbar was angered by the obstinate defence
and showed none of the generosity he usually

exhibited to the conquered. Thousands were massacred in the city by his order.

Heretofore, no invader had succeeded in subduing the proud Rajputs in their fastnesses. The fall of Chitor, the renowned and sacred fortress, and the slaughter that followed it, were never to be forgotten by the Rajput race. But on the Mogul side a profound impression was made by the heroic resistance: and Akbar caused two statues to be made of Jaimall and of the young prince Patta, a boy of sixteen, who, with his mother and his bride, all fighting, perished in the defence of Chitor. They were set up at Delhi.

VIII

WITH all his achievements Akbar lacked and greatly longed for a thing which fortune had so far denied him. He had scores of wives, but he had no son. There had been twins, but both had died in infancy. He made pilgrimages to holy shrines and offered up many prayers, but he was still denied what to men like him, craving a successor to continue his work, is the crowning boon of life. There was a certain ascetic who had his hut among the rocks at Sikri, some score of miles from Agra, called Shaikh Salim, and he prophesied to the emperor that his prayers would be granted and that three sons would be born to him. And when Akbar heard with joy that his Rajput wife, the daughter of the Rajah of Jaipur, was with child, he sent her to Sikri that she might be delivered there, where the saint of happy prophecy had his dwelling. At the end of August 1569 a boy was born and received the name Salim after the saint. In June of the following year a second son was born, the child of a concubine, and was called Murad. Akbar

65

rejoiced exceedingly. Could he have foreseen his sons' future, his joy would have been tempered.

It was in commemoration of the birth of his sons in that spot, now sacred in his eyes, that Akbar now designed to build there a new capital. The building of the city was begun forthwith and carried on for about fourteen years. So mosques and palaces arose, and schools and baths and gardens, and a circus for polo and elephant-fights, and a wall of red sandstone built round the city; and an artificial lake, six miles long, formed to provide water for it. And after the conquest of Gujerat, the city was called Fatehpur-Sikri, the City of Victory. On the great portal of the mosque was the famous inscription: 'So said Jesus, upon whom be peace. The world is a bridge; pass over it, but build no house upon it.'

It seemed as if wall and tower could not rise fast enough to keep pace with Akbar's furious energy. Like Timur at Samarcand, he would stand over the throngs of builders and artificers, urging them on, supervising every detail of the work at once. Building possessed him like a passion. He eyed the blocks of red sandstone with an eye that penetrated through them to the shapes, already in his mind, of column, lintel, cornice. At times, nothing would content him but he must quarry the stone himself, along with the other workmen. So the buildings rose with fantastic speed. It was as if Akbar heard always at his back 'Time's winged chariot hurrying near'; as if some premonition warned him that all his magnificence was perishable, that the hour would come when the words inscribed on the great portal of the mosque would sound like the sentence of Fate, and all his labour of creation appear as the fabric of a dream. After being a chief centre of Asiatic culture, one of the most brilliant cities of its time in the world, it was to be abandoned by its creator as suddenly as it had been conceived and planned. Was it because it proved unhealthy, or because the water supply failed? Perhaps: but it is just as likely that it was for some reason that was no reason, some superstitious instinct or some unaccountable prompting from within, which drove Akbar to his sudden resolution.

An English traveller, one of the first to reach India, has described it as 'much greater than London' and very populous, 'a great resort of merchants from Persia and out of India, and very much merchandise of silk and cloth, and of precious stones, both Rubies, Diamonds, and Pearls.' But when Ralph Fitch passed through Fatehpur-Sikri, it was on the very eve of its desertion; for Akbar, who held his court there from 1569, left it in 1585 and never, save for one brief visit, returned. In 1604 Father Jerome Xavier, of the Third Jesuit mission, passed through the city and found it 'totally demolished' save for the great buildings made by the emperor. The swarming population had abandoned it: the streets were empty. The City of Victory was a city of desolation, left to the jackals and the bats. 'Here, we might say,' wrote Xavier, 'stood Troy.'

But in the early days of its splendour, Fatehpur-Sikri rivalled or surpassed Herat in the time of Baisunqur in its assemblage of architects and painters and calligraphers, poets and musicians and philosophers, and might almost recall, were it not for the difference in quality, the feverish intellectual and creative activity of the cities of Italy in the heyday of the Renaissance. Only, just as the city itself was the sudden embodiment, created at fabulous expenditure, of a single imperious will, so this brilliant and busy centre of the various arts had in it a certain element of artificiality. As the barren ledges of rock had been transformed into palaces and gardens with stretches of shining

68

water, and as the flowers had been sown in the
gardens, and trees planted in the alleys, so artists
had been collected from all quarters and settled in the palaces and workshops, and bidden
to flourish and create. There was no local
root of tradition, no gradual flowering from the
soil.

Not that Akbar lacked sensibility, or was
merely bent on self-glorification. He came of a
race in which a restless and stormy life could
not dull the taste for art and letters. He does
not indeed seem to have had the extraordinary
sensibility to beauty in nature which is so remarkable in Babur; but in his feeling for art
there was infused a semi-religious sentiment.
His son Jahangir was to be the typical patron,
collector, connoisseur: but to Akbar art was
an avenue to the glory of the creative world and
a means of apprehending the Creator. He himself had learned to draw as a boy when Humayun had brought the Persian artists to Kabul:
and those two Persian masters were the chiefs
of his school. Gradually, however, Hindu
artists were attracted to the court and came
quite to outnumber the Persians. The Indian
style absorbed the Persian, and a new school
began to flourish: a school almost entirely of
portraiture and illustration, delighting in ani-

mated and crowded scenes, in dramatic motives. One notices how fond these painters are of figures in running movement; as if Akbar had communicated to them his own exuberant energy. Not a great art, perhaps; but since there were no artists of supreme gift, how much better that they should be employed in vivid portrayal of the contemporary scene than in heroic and ideal compositions! How often we are moved to deplore that in Europe gifts adequate to portraiture have wasted themselves in misguided ambition! Through these artists we see, at any rate, Akbar as he lived, fought, hunted, prayed; and all his surroundings.

Yet art was not Akbar's dominant passion or chief recreation: and all this artistic production was after all but a department of the multifarious activity of the capital. Amid the bustle of active men, the come-and-go of soldiers, politicians and adventurers, the concourse of administrative officers, the artists, though treated with favour and regard, could hardly have felt themselves to be the recognised glory of the city; in the world of great affairs, of which Fatehpur-Sikri was the pulsating centre, they counted for little. The atmosphere resembled that of imperial Rome rather than that of Florence in the time of Lorenzo the Magnificent: a post-meridian atmosphere, not the morning fervour which abounds in glorious promise yet to be fulfilled. Akbar's artists looked back to no struggling primitives behind them, but to the finished achievements, supreme in this kind, of the Persian masters. And his patronage would have resulted in less of value had it not been for the example and opportunity it gave for revivals of the indigenous schools of Indian art in local centres. The Hindu element, after his death, came to infiltrate more and more the Mogul school, while outside the capital provincial rajahs encouraged artists to give fresh life to ancient native traditions. The whole Mogul school reflects Akbar's political aspirations: its aim is to fuse the Persian, the Muhammadan, with the Hindu style.

Having the Persians as their models, the Mogul school at this period devoted themselves chiefly to the adornment of manuscripts. And here the penmanship was even more valued than the painting. Akbar valued his fine calligraphers, and, though he could not write himself, he could distinguish and appreciate. A subordinate army of binders and gilders worked under the painters and calligraphers. At his death Akbar had a library of 24,000 volumes, all in manuscript, many with costly illuminations. There were weekly inspections, at which the emperor gave rewards and adjusted salaries. But the painters were not only called on to produce small portraits and book-illustrations; there were frescoes to be painted on the walls of public buildings, though these unfortunately have almost entirely perished. The buildings remain, and in the architecture is the most splendid monument of Akbar's magnificence. The planning of Fatehpur-Sikri was his own.

Frequently Akbar would pass from his palace to the adjoining workshops where the painters, the goldsmiths, the tapestry-makers, the carpet weavers, and the armourers were at work, and watch them with keen enjoyment. And from there he would return to his palace and mingle with the groups of learned men, theologians and poets. It is true that the greatest poet of his time, Tulsi Das, the author of the Hindi epic *Ramayan,* and one of the greatest names in Indian literature, seems to have been unknown to Akbar. He lived and died at Benares. But this can hardly have been from any conscious neglect.

IX

AKBAR'S aim was to rule from sea to sea. His eyes were now turned westward. There, between the frontiers of his dominions and the Arabian Sea, lay Gujerat, a province not only desirable in itself, for the sea-borne trade enriched its markets, but now conveniently unsettled and in need of a strong government. Muzaffar Shah was the nominal king, but had little control over a number of minor chieftains, one of whom made overtures to the emperor. An additional pretext for the expedition now planned was the fact that the country had once been occupied for a time by Humayun. The capital, Ahmadabad, was a wealthy and important city: 'Very neare as big as London,' it is described a little later by an English traveller, with many merchants in cloth of gold, taffetas, and other fabrics.

Starting in July 1572 from Fatehpur-Sikri, Akbar sent on ahead a force of ten thousand men. News of the birth of a third son, Daniyal, cheered him on the march. All at first went smoothly. Muzaffar Shah hid from the imperial presence in a cornfield, and when discovered made his submission. Akbar regarded his success as assured, formally annexed the country, and proceeded, with his usual energy, to superintend the details of administration.

He had hitherto never set eyes on the sea. It is a little singular that there is no record of the impression the experience when at Cambay he first saw and sailed upon the ocean which connected India with Europe. It was now that he first met with Portuguese traders from the West. 'In the harbour of Cambay might be seen,' says the English traveller I have already quoted, 'as many as two hundred frigates at once.' The emperor's curiosity was doubtless aroused, but no thought of the possibilities of sea-power seems to have entered his head.

While Akbar was absent at Cambay, there was a sudden revolt, headed by his kinsman Ibrahim Husain Mirza. With a large force the insurgents held a small town called Sarnal on the Mahi River. No sooner had Akbar heard the news than he dashed off in haste and fury. When he arrived before Sarnal he had but two hundred horse with him, but insisted on attacking at once. The river was forded, the horses impelled up the steep bank opposite, and the enemy's far superior force engaged. It was a wild encounter among hedges of cactus, in which the combatants became entangled: a hand-to-hand fight, where personal prowess only counted. Akbar, riding with Bhagwan Das, was assailed by three of the enemy. Two he drove off; Bhagwan Das sent a spear-thrust through the third. Meanwhile the rest of Akbar's force had come up, and, as night came on, the enemy fled. Ibrahim escaped; he was to be taken later in the Punjab, where he had sought a refuge, and died of wounds.

Early in the new year, Akbar laid siege to the port of Surat, which was held by the Mirzas. Soon he learnt that they were being assisted by the Portuguese, and made overtures through an envoy to the Viceroy, who sent Antonio Cabral to the emperor. The negotiations ended in a peace being concluded. Surat capitulated at the end of February 1573. In April Akbar started back, and arrived in his capital in June.

Apart from curiosity, the emperor had his reasons for entering into relations with the Portuguese. Probably at the back of his mind was the desire to oust these Europeans from India altogether. But that, if a hope to be cherished, could not yet be a settled intention. He wished first to know more about the Por-

tuguese and their power. Their superior artillery was always to be his envy. At this time,
being an orthodox Muhammadan, he was solici-
tous about the pilgrims from India to Mecca,
who could only cross the Arabian Sea on
Portuguese ships and who were subjected to in-
dignities much resented. They were obliged to
procure passports stamped with images of the
Virgin Mary and of Jesus; and the passports
were costly. Tom Coryat, that unwearied and
irrepressible vagabond, the butt of the wits of
the Mermaid Tavern, who travelled alone and
mostly on foot from London to the Mogul's
dominions (arriving a little after Akbar's
death), tells a story that the Portuguese had once
tied a Koran round a dog's neck and beaten the
dog through the streets of Ormuz; in revenge
for which Akbar's mother implored him to have
a Bible hung about a donkey's neck and beaten
round the town. But Akbar refused: it did
not become him to take revenge on an innocent book, or to requite ill for ill. Whether
the story be fact or no, certain it is that Akbar
was already interested in Christianity, and
whenever he came into personal contact with
the Portuguese inquired about the doctrines of
this religion. At the present stage curiosity,
not only about religion but about the customs

and political institutions of the Western peoples, was the dominant motive in his mind.

Having then returned in apparent triumph to his capital, and having treated the prisoners taken with an unaccustomed and cruel severity, Akbar was preparing to throw himself into new occupations. Suddenly news was brought that after all Gujerat, so happily conquered, was again in rebellion. Without a moment's hesitation Akbar decided on a fresh campaign. If the first expedition had shown him in his glory as a fighting-man, leading his soldiers with the reckless daring of an Alexander, this second expedition reveals him as the born general. Surprised as he was, and resolved that instant action was imperative, he left nothing to chance, inspected every detail, and, as much unforeseen expenditure was necessary, drew largely on his own purse for funds.

In the fierce heat of August he started with a small force of about three thousand cavalry. Across Rajputana he raced at the rate of fifty miles a day. In eleven days he was again before Ahmadabad, having covered a distance of six hundred miles. The rebels, headed by Muhammad Husain Mirza, numbered about twenty thousand. They were astounded by the appearance of the imperial force. 'What,' they said, 'the emperor? But our spies have told us that he was at Fatehpur-Sikri a fortnight ago. It is impossible that he should be here by now.' Their astonishment was soon to change to consternation. Akbar, as usual, attacked at once. He crossed the river before the town. There was a check. The small vanguard recoiled before superior numbers. Then appeared Akbar, who charged 'like a tiger.' His horse was wounded. The rumour flew about that he was killed. He mounted a fresh horse. He was seen again in the forefront of the battle, and his troops, recovering from this momentary dismay, rallied, cheering. It was the moment which decides a battle. The enemy gave way; Muhammad Husain was wounded and captured; the day was won. Yet not at once. For before an hour had passed another of the rebel leaders with a force of five thousand emerged from the other side of the city and made an attempt to reverse disaster. But the sudden and unexpected rout of the main body communicated a panic. Confronted with the apparition of the victorious Akbar and his little army, they were bewildered and hardly had the wits to flee. Such a panic seized them that they let their enemies pull the arrows out of the quivers at their backs and use their own weapons against them. Victory was complete. According to the ancient and horrible custom of Timur, which was still honoured by Akbar, a pyramid of two thousand severed heads was piled up on the field of battle, for, as we have seen, Akbar the warrior was far more subservient to tradition than Akbar the ruler, and the observances of his ancestors in war seemed to have acquired for him a sort of sanctity.

Gujerat needed no third lesson. It was conquered finally. The return journey was made in three weeks. The whole campaign had occupied forty-three days.

It has been said, no doubt with truth, that the armies led by Akbar were of poor quality as a military instrument, and could have had no chance against disciplined European troops. If so, we can but admire the skilful use he made of them. Whatever his material, he displayed the essential qualities of a great commander: he was a master of swiftness and surprise. Never were these qualities so brilliantly shown as on this amazing brief campaign.

X

IN the spring of 1574 there arrived at court a young man who was destined to a brilliant career; who was to become Akbar's closest and most trusted friend, and to write the history of his achievements.

Abul Fazl was the son of a Shaikh, Mubarak, who was himself notable alike for his learning and unorthodox opinions. The year 1591-92 was the year, now not so far off, which would complete the first millennium of Islam. Such is the hypnotic effect of numbers on the human mind that, just as had happened in the Buddhist, and later in the Christian Church, the completion of a thousand years was looked forward to with much agitation, and some dramatic event was by many expected with confidence. In the Muhammadan world the event so looked for was the coming of a 'Mahdi,' a prophet who was to restore the clouded faith of Islam to its pristine freshness. Mubarak was attached to this religious movement, which also influenced Akbar and strengthened the growing revolt in his mind against the frigid bigotry

of the orthodox teachers. Mubarak had suffered persecution at the hands of the official
doctors of the law; both his liberalism and the
intolerance it provoked predisposed the emperor in his favour. Moreover, it was he who,
when Akbar returned from the first Gujerat
campaign, had gone out to meet him, and had
urged the emperor to become not only the
temporal but the spiritual head of his subjects:
and this pregnant suggestion was never forgotten. His two sons, of whom Abul Fazl was
the younger, shared their father's views; both
shone in boyhood with precocious promise:
Faizi, the elder, as a poet, Abul Fazl as a scholar.
It was during the siege of Chitor, in 1567, that
Faizi first presented himself to the emperor and
was cordially treated: he was to become, some
twenty years later, Akbar's Laureate. Abul
Fazl was introduced to the emperor by his
brother; and Akbar took notice of him from the
first. According to his own account, he was consumed with a longing to retire from the world,
yet attracted, moth-like, by the glory of his
sovereign. One day in a mosque he was medi-
tating when Akbar happened to enter: and to
his surprise and delight he was recognised and
spoken to. This was the beginning of many
favours. Akbar found Abul Fazl a man after

his own heart. He was a courtier born. Moreover, his was an alert and flexible intelligence.
Among all the courtiers the Jesuits, competent
judges, found Abul Fazl pre-eminent in qualities of mind. It is true that he is a tedious
writer. It is often a little difficult to disengage
the facts recorded in the *Akbar-namah,* so over-
grown are they with Persian flowers of speech:
still the facts are there. Abul Fazl was even
capable of commanding an army and conduct-
ing a campaign with more success than some
of Akbar's generals. At this period, however,
he was a young, enthusiastic student, with an
immense admiration for the emperor, who saw
in him an invaluable ally and support in his
religious adventures.

It was at the same time that another person
came to court who, like Abul Fazl, was also to
be Akbar's historian. But from a very different
point of view. Badaoni was of the straitest sect
of Muslims. He was to witness with secret but
increasing wrath the emperor's lapses from the
faith, and his comments grew bitterer every
year: so that it became impossible for his history to be published till after Akbar was dead.

But just now Akbar was obliged to postpone
the religious discussions which he had at heart
and in which both these young men took, from

their opposite points of view, so deep an interest. For if, to Badaoni, the spirit of inquiry was in itself reprehensible as tending to unsettle belief, he was deeply concerned nevertheless in his master's activities. But once more a revolt had broken out, and a great expedition was being busily prepared.

This time the scene of war was Bengal. A young prince called Daud had been placed on the throne of Bengal, which, with Bihar, was held by Afghan chiefs. Finding himself master of a huge army and immense treasure, he decided that he was strong enough to defy Akbar, and seized a frontier fort. Akbar was then in Gujerat. He sent orders to Munim Khan, an aged and now tired general, to punish Daud. But Munim failed to do anything decisive; and at last, having sat down before Patna to lay siege to it, he felt unable to do more and besought the emperor to come himself. And Akbar came.

This was a new kind of campaign: for the Ganges was to be used for transport. Akbar sent part of his forces by land, but with the rest embarked on a fleet of great boats. The villagers on the banks were astonished to see these vessels with their crimson sails crowding the broad river; some carried elephants, others a variety of paraphernalia, others had been converted into gardens with scented flowers and foliage. From such pomp and luxury, whoever might have predicted an indolent and ornamental expedition would have been greatly mistaken. For in this campaign Akbar was to show the contempt of a Frederick or a Napoleon for time-honoured military observances. It was against all rules of Indian warfare that a campaign should be conducted in the rainy season; and great was the disgust and annoyance among the enemy when they heard that the imperial troops were advancing rapidly against them without the least regard for torrential rains and flooded rivers. This alarm increased with every day that brought Akbar nearer. He arrived before Patna; took the city with enormous booty: and Daud fled. Munim, Todar Mall, and other generals were left to finish the campaign, while Akbar returned to Fatehpur-Sikri.

As he travelled homeward his thoughts were full of a project which he determined at once to carry into execution. This was to build a 'House of Worship' wherein were to assemble learned doctors representing all schools of thought in Islam and to join in those discussions which had for him so intoxicating an attraction. Rapidly, under his eager orders, the building rose, and soon the walls resounded with the buzz of many voices in ardent disputation. Nor at first was the disputation only on abstract themes: questions of seating and precedence occupied the jostling sages. So it was ordained that on the south side should sit the Learned Doctors; on the north, the Ascetics and Mystics; on the west, reputed descendants of the Prophet; on the east, such Nobles as cared for these matters. And Akbar presided over them all: not enthroned in immovable dignity, but moving in his restless way freely among them, and talking now with one and now with another.

Interminable were the disputes among the innumerable sects of Islam. Akbar was in his element; he loved to listen to discussions like those with which Milton's angels amused their eternal leisure.

But before long a sense of dissatisfaction came upon him. He became satiated with the pretentious learning and labyrinthine arguments of the Doctors, and satiety deepened to disgust.

I think there is no doubt that Akbar, a man who to all things brought the test of conduct and experience, judged of religions far less by their abstract tenets than by their fruits in the life of those professing them. And only a year after the House of Worship had risen in its bright newness, a certain piece of news was brought to the capital which greatly impressed him. The first two Christian missionaries had arrived in Bengal. Their converts had defrauded the imperial revenue: the priests thereon refused them absolution. What was this creed which set its face against dishonesty even to a foreign government? Akbar was seized with his inveterate curiosity (he had indeed made inquiries before about the Christian creed, but had gained but little information), and in 1578 sent for the Vicar-General in Bengal, Father Pereira, and questioned him. But Pereira, more pious than learned, felt helpless under the emperor's battery of questions, and advised that some one more learned than himself should be sent for. There were plenty such among the Jesuits. So it came about that a letter (the text is extant) was despatched to Goa, asking for two learned priests to be sent to Fatehpur-Sikri. After much hesitation, the invitation was accepted. Ridolfo Aquaviva, a young Neapolitan Jesuit, of noble family, newly arrived at Goa, was chosen as chief of the mission: with him was sent Antonio Monserrate, a Spaniard, who was to write the full story of the mission. Henriquez, a Persian convert from Islam, also went with them.

It has been charged against Akbar that in inviting the Jesuits to his court he was playing a perfidious part, since he really regarded the Portuguese as his enemies and hoped one day to drive them from their settlements on the Indian coast. No doubt there were for him political advantages in getting into touch with these Europeans and learning about their resources and their aims; and in his dealings with Goa he was certainly guilty at times of duplicity. But it seems to me impossible to believe that he was not perfectly genuine in his desire to know the nature and the doctrines of Christianity, or that his friendship with the Jesuit envoys was insincere. By his cordial reception of them he went far towards risking, not only his throne, but his life. What possible political advantage could counterbalance the danger at home to which, with great pertinacity and against violent opposition, he insisted on exposing himself? But it was quite in his character, while indulging his insatiable interest in religion for its own sake, not to neglect the means of pursuing at the same time other ends for political profit.

Meanwhile Akbar had gone through another

of those strange experiences of the spirit which had marked his youth and early manhood.

In April 1578 one of those enormous hunts or *kamargahs* on a fantastic scale, in which sometimes as many as fifty thousand beaters were employed, had been ordered in the Punjab. The game was driven in from a ring measuring forty or fifty miles in circumference. For ten days the beaters had been at work preparing for the monstrous slaughter which consummated the proceedings, when suddenly and without warning all was imperiously stopped. No one was 'to touch the feather of a finch,' and every animal was to be let escape according to its habits.

What had happened? The sombre Badaoni says that 'a strange state and strong frenzy came upon the Emperor,' which one ascribed to this cause and one to another, but 'God alone knoweth secrets.' Mr. Vincent Smith, robust in common sense, opines that perhaps he slept and had a dream or, more probably, an epileptic fit.

Abul Fazl's account, clothed in roseate rhetoric though it be, is, I think, more worthy of belief. To Akbar on this day of May, as on that other day long ago when, a boy, he had spurred out into the solitude of the plain, came once more a moment of intense illumination. He had the sense of union with God. In that moment a vast revulsion overcame him from all his tremendous activities in the world, from his earthly pomp and splendour, nay, from his very throne. How much better to abdicate it all; to be, like the humble hermits, alone with the light of the mind. In such a moment of exaltation the thought of the huge and horrible massacre of unoffending animals that was preparing seemed suddenly a frightful and stupid crime. For all life, in the Creator's eyes, was one. It was under a tree where he was resting, as two thousand years earlier it had been with the Buddha, that the moment of illumination came to Akbar.

But once again, when the ecstasy had departed, the imperious demands of state affairs, the habit of activity, the needs of the exuberant body, recaptured this soul from its errancy into the infinite. Akbar was once more the emperor, the unwearied worker, the guardian of his people. In the intervals of leisure he resorted again to the House of Worship; but this had by now become the tumultuous scene of the most acrimonious disputation. Two rival sects were in bitter opposition, each claiming to possess the only truth. But who can be sure that he is right? Akbar's thoughts always returned to this question. The confident bigotry of these Muslims was a thing inconceivable to himself; and the more positive they became, the more he doubted. Islam was parading before him all that he least admired, and ended by estranging him altogether.

But where was the truth, which he so longed to find? Perhaps if members of other faiths were invited to the debates, something might emerge and be discovered. All religions were made welcome; and beside the sects of Islam, the Sunnis, the Shias, and the Sufis, might now be seen Hindus, Jains, Parsees, Zoroastrians, Jews, and finally Christians.

For in February of 1580, after some months of travel, Aquaviva and his companions at last arrived. They were astonished at the magnificence of the capital. As they passed through the streets every one stopped to stare at these strange people, robed in black, with shaven faces and tonsured hair, and unarmed. Strange figures they appeared, too, at their first audience of the emperor, so plain and austere among the Mogul grandees with their ropes of pearls, their silken dresses, and air of splendour. An artist of Akbar's court has portrayed the scene. Aquaviva, short-sighted, untidy, and absent-minded—he was always looking for his mislaid hat or spectacles—was so shy that he blushed when called on to reply to the emperor or address him. But he had a hero's soul. Elated beyond measure at the Heaven-accorded opportunity of converting this mighty potentate, he secretly cherished one desire only, to win the crown of martyrdom. When will they martyr us? he would sigh, weary of being protected and caressed.

Akbar received the Jesuits kindly and ordered a large present of money to be given them. This was of course refused, and the refusal was repeated. Akbar admired such self-control; so new to his experience. Before attempting the desired conversion, the Fathers sounded Pereira as to the emperor's attitude towards Christianity. It appeared that Akbar had the utmost reverence for Christ and delighted in the Gospel: but when he heard that there are three Persons in one God, and that God had begotten a son from a virgin, then 'the king's judgment was dulled and clouded.' Also the forbidding a man to have more than one wife seemed very strange; decidedly inconvenient to a monarch with three hundred wives in his harem. However, he spoke very slightingly of Muhammad: and this at least was a good sign.

So it was not without hope that they attended Akbar's summons, bringing with them as a present a Bible written in four languages and bound in seven volumes. Akbar kissed it and placed it on his head. Next, the Fathers were invited to debate with the doctors of Islam.

The first discussions were on the Koran, with which the Jesuits were well acquainted in a Latin translation; and this unexpected familiarity both astonished Akbar and disconcerted the Muslims. They ended with a challenge by the Muhammadans to an ordeal by fire. One of them, carrying the Koran, and one of the Christians, carrying the Bible, were to walk through a fire; and the book which passed through the fire unharmed was to be adjudged true. The priests replied that their faith needed no miracles to confirm it: but afterwards Aquaviva sought out the emperor privately and said they were quite willing to ascend the pyre, if he ordered them, though they did not expect any miracle to be performed on their behalf. Then Akbar, who had in public urged them to accept the ordeal, confided to Aquaviva that he had a secret motive of his own. There was a certain Mullah, who professed great sanctity but was really a depraved, wicked fellow: and Akbar's design was

that this man should mount the pyre and perish
in the flames. He apparently anticipated no
miraculous intervention, at any rate on behalf
of the Koran. Aquaviva replied that priests
were forbidden not only 'to take life but even
to help to bring about a man's execution or
death.' 'But,' said Akbar, 'I don't want you
to undergo the ordeal, only to say that you are
willing.'

'We can't do even that.'

'Well, then, consent to this. I will announce
that you will pass through the fire. You shall
be silent.'

'If you do so, we shall as publicly announce
that we will do no such thing. If this man
deserves punishment, why not punish him in
a straightforward manner, instead of by this
tortuous device?'

Such is Monserrate's account of this strange
incident. Abul Fazl says that it was the Jesuits
who proposed the ordeal, and that the mean-
spirited Mullahs had only angry words in
answer. Badaoni, on the other hand, asserts
that the fire was made (and in an illustration to
one of the MSS. of the *Akbar-namah* the scene
is depicted with the fire in the midst of the disputants), and that a Shaikh pulled one of the
Fathers by the coat and dared him to enter it,

but he had not the courage. I think Monserrate is the most worthy of credence. It is plain that Akbar had no real belief in the efficacy of the ordeal, though he had enough of superstition in him (it comes out on other occasions) to wish perhaps to put it to the test. And even the singular and rather childish plan for getting rid of a Mullah whom he disliked and distrusted, a plan which seemed so base and disingenuous to Aquaviva, may well have appealed to his grim sense of humour. It seems that the challenge was repeated more than once, but never came to anything.

Akbar was impressed with the transparent honesty and outspokenness of Aquaviva; he came to esteem and like him more and more. But he was in a difficult and delicate position. It seems wonderful indeed that his falling away from the creed of his ancestors, a creed so inflexible and intolerant of all rivals, should have been accepted without more open resentment than was shown. Alarm, distrust, and bitter feeling it certainly evoked in all the Muhammadans. To some extent, no doubt, the fierce disputes among their many sects weakened the effectiveness of their opposition. Moreover, Akbar's throne was buttressed by the Hindus, to whom he had given posts of trust and authority. He was backed by Abul Fazl and men of his way of thinking, though these were few. But Akbar's main reliance was on his own personal ascendancy.

Christianity did not, however, appeal to him so much on further acquaintance.. Probably if Aquaviva and Monserrate had been men of a different stamp, and not the honest and devoted men they were, Akbar would have soon ceased to coquet with the creed they sought to bring him to. But it was evident that they wished to take sole charge of him, and meant, if he would let them, entirely to subdue his mind and will to theirs. They were determined that he should first change his way of life and put away all his wives save one, and also give up far more time to private instruction at their hands and curtail the hours devoted to business and sport. This he had no mind to do at all. But for the moment he told them that, deeply as he reverenced the Gospel and the person of Christ, he could not understand the doctrines of the Trinity and the Virgin Birth, and while he remained without this understanding he could not accept in its fulness the Christian religion. To which, of course, Aquaviva replied that he must pray for enlightenment and humble his intellect before the power of faith.

From the first Akbar had occasion to warn the Fathers to be cautious with the Muhammadan leaders and not too violent in their denunciations of the Prophet. They were indeed outspoken to a degree, but tried to be moderate in their behaviour, though their feelings were outraged on every hand by the homage paid to the 'infernal monster' Muhammad. In a letter to the Rector of Goa, Aquaviva writes that 'We cannot speak the truth out, lest, if we go too far, we endanger the life of the King.'

Here, then, was a most complex situation. On the one side, Aquaviva, still young and inexperienced in the world's ways—he was not thirty when he arrived at Goa—delicate in health but inflexible of will, a natural saint, to whom had appeared the glorious vision of converting to the Faith this magnificent and mighty monarch in a vast country of the infidels which as yet knew nothing of the Gospel; but though actually installed in the palace (for after Easter on Akbar's invitation the Jesuits moved thither from their uncomfortable inn) and received with gracious welcome and all manner of kindness, finding an impalpable veil between him and the soul he longed to win.

On the other side, Akbar, living the life of ten men at once, holding all the threads of the government of a vast dominion in his own hands, committed to an incessant and multifarious activity, both bodily and mental; how, without abdicating, without denying all the instincts of his being, could he yield himself into the hands of one who demanded complete submission and the utter change of all his ways? And Aquaviva, who lived for his religion and that alone, who loved solitude, who mortified his flesh continually with fasting and self-flagellation, who comforted his spirit with the singing of little songs which he improvised to the honour and glory of the Virgin, who longed for release by martyrdom—how could Aquaviva understand? Mutually attracted as human beings, they were in reality worlds apart.

XI

THE real mind of Akbar was perhaps disclosed when, summoning the priests to a private audience, he declared of his own accord that he wished the Christians to come and live freely in his empire, and build their churches where they willed, just as he allowed the Hindus to build their temples unmolested. The Fathers were so struck with this spontaneous declaration, spoken with such 'love and kindliness,' that Aquaviva postponed an address which he had prepared to his imperial pupil, the tenor of which was most uncompromising. Akbar seems genuinely to have been afraid of assassination on account of his heterodoxy; he hinted this, and explained that if he were killed, his dynasty would perish and his empire crumble. He must therefore move warily and slowly.

The Jesuits on their part felt that they too must be circumspect and not push their cause too urgently at first. One cannot imagine that what Akbar proposed to them was anything but disappointing and distasteful; that is, if this were all he had to offer. At this stage, no doubt, it seemed a token of conciliation, and more might come of it: but they were for all or nothing. Either Akbar would be converted, an immense and resounding triumph for the Church, or they would turn their backs on his court and go back to Goa. To be put on a level with the idolaters, as they always termed the Hindus, was humiliating: a concession that might be turned to great advantage, but by no means what they had been led to hope.

Yet such a concession as this was all that Akbar had to offer. He saw good men professing various creeds; there must be good in all of them, he argued. A sympathetic toleration in religious matters was his settled policy. It was the intolerance of the Muslims which had repelled him and turned him away from the faith of his forefathers. And now in the Christians he found an intolerance of equal intensity and force. This, more than anything else, we may surmise, prevented him from accepting Christianity, if ever the thought really held his mind.

But if he would not accept, neither would he reject. He encouraged; he conciliated; but just when it seemed that he was at the point to promise all and submit himself, he eluded them. And yet how far he went! He would often

spend half the night with the Fathers, questioning, debating, and seeking instruction.
Aquaviva on his part begged for a Persian
teacher, and in a few months was so proficient
in the language that he was able to translate
parts of the Gospels and to dispute with the
Muslims in their own tongue. But what raised
the greatest hopes was Akbar's giving the
Jesuits charge of his second son Murad, for
education was ever the means on which their
order most relied.

They made friends with Abul Fazl, who delighted in their company and gave them strong
support, just as he was the emperor's chief
abettor in his policy of toleration throughout
the empire. And feeling now on securer
ground, the Fathers did not hesitate to rebuke
the emperor with great frankness for some of
his proclivities, and for certain things which he
permitted in his realm. They refused to attend
a gladiatorial show; they protested vehemently
against a *suttee* which they were invited to witness; they admonished him on the wickedness
of letting his sons be corrupted by the teachings
of Islam. Akbar showed no resentment. Indeed, he refused thenceforth to attend a *suttee*,
which infuriated the Brahmans. He conversed
with them familiarly and without ceremony;

would pace up and down with his arm round Aquaviva's shoulder. They had the entry into the innermost parts of the palace, and would have been overwhelmed with gifts had they allowed themselves to accept them. In short, such was the favour shown to the priests that the hostility of the Muhammadans became more and more outspoken; and the rumour was spread abroad that Akbar was on the point of embracing Christianity. The orthodox, wherever the rumour ran, became restless: the ambitious saw in the deplorable laxity of the emperor an opportunity for rising against him. The opposition on the part of Akbar's wives was not less powerful because not publicly shown. To them Christianity was a pernicious creed, with its odious principle of monogamy. It was inconceivable, or at least lamentable to conceive, that the emperor should adopt this foreign faith and be induced to discard at a blow all his wives. Still more atrocious would it be were he forced to the invidiousness of choosing one. Truly, Akbar was in no enviable position.

The accounts given by the Jesuits of Akbar and of his attitude to Christianity are so full and intimate, written moreover by acute observers of high intelligence, that we may easily be led into laying a disproportinate emphasis on their influence over his mind. If he was attracted to the religion of Christ, he was not less attracted by the doctrines of the Jains and by the ancient Persian faith of Zoroaster, while he also followed the Hindus in some at least of their observances. To Islam alone he became by degrees definitely hostile.

Had we equally full accounts from those who instructed him in the various creeds, we should, no doubt, see Akbar behaving in the same manner as he did to the Jesuits, though perhaps none appealed to him so much by their personal character. With each religion he went so far that each in turn claimed him as a convert, or as being about to be converted: in each case he stopped upon the threshold.

Of all these religions it is probable that Zoroastrianism had the strongest hold on his mind. Dastur Meher-ji Rana, a Parsee theologian from Gujerat, whom he first met at the siege of Surat in 1573, played the part of Aquaviva. He was summoned to court, and Akbar was initiated by him into the Zoroastrian mysteries.

It would seem that Akbar, in his restless seeking for a faith that should satisfy his inner nature, never contented himself with abstract inquiries, but as if determined to put on the whole habit of a creed, and to taste its efficacy from the inside, adopted with each its outward ceremony and ritual, and used its symbols, all apparently with a like sincerity of approach.

So, since the Zoroastrian faith centres round the worship of the sun, a sacred fire, never to be extinguished, was kindled in the palace. It was committed to the charge of Abul Fazl. And from the beginning of the twenty-fifth year of Akbar's reign the emperor began the custom of prostrating himself solemnly and in public before the sun. When in the evening the lamps were lighted, the whole court were required to rise in honour of what Akbar himself called 'a commemoration of the sunrise.' It is a singular thing that this public adoption of Parsee rites took place in March 1580, a month after the arrival of the Jesuits. But they apparently were so absorbed in contending against the Muhammadans that Akbar's fire-worship was not remarked on; or they did not take it seriously. Yet it is likely that the simplicity of the Zoroastrian symbolism made a strong appeal to Akbar's mind, with its tendency to mysticism, its dislike of complicated doctrines and hatred of bigotry. It is characteristic of him that while he was engaging the Jesuits in such frequent talk and earnest inquiry into Christian doctrine, he was all the time encouraging, and himself practising, the Zoroastrian ritual.

Yet another religion was to occupy his attention and to exert considerable influence on his life. This was the religion of the Jains. That religion is almost, if not quite, as old as Buddhism. And, like Buddhism, it arose as a revolt against the Brahmans. Its chief tenet was the absolute prohibition of the taking of any life, whether human or animal. From the year 1578 two or three Jain teachers were always at the court. The chief of these, Hiravijaya, played a part, in relation to Akbar, similar to that of Aquaviva.

With the Sikh religion also the emperor had some contact, and though it did not influence him he treated the Sikhs with sympathy and favour. The Brahmans complained of them, and Akbar, as usual, was eager to have a discussion between them, but the proposal was not accepted. The Sikh Guru Arjun was accused of treating with contempt both Muslim prophets and Hindu gods. Akbar however found in his writings nothing but love and devotion to God: they were, he said, 'worthy of reverence.'

XII

SHAH MANSUR was a petty clerk who showed a remarkable aptitude for accounts and the details of finance. Akbar noticed his ability and raised him to high office. He became the Finance Minister of the empire. A genius for figures, a punctilious exactingness, and a heart of stone made him an ideal Treasury official: and his love of money added zest to his efficiency. The recently conquered provinces of Bengal and Bihar were in a state of irritation over certain unpopular orders, particularly that concerning the branding of horses for government service. Shah Mansur insisted on their strict enforcement; he also cut down, on his own responsibility, allowances of pay. Sore at these and other grievances, the Muhammadans in Bengal were now also alarmed by Akbar's religious innovations and his growing alienation from Islam. Disaffection grew to open rebellion, which a daring theologian pronounced to be lawful against an heretical emperor. The chiefs of the insurrection turned their eyes to Kabul, where Akbar's younger half-brother was governor. What matter that Muhammad Hakim was a drunken weakling? He was orthodox. It was planned to bring him into the conspiracy and place him on the throne. The rebellion had broken out at the beginning of 1580, and by 1581 was by no means crushed. Secret negotiations were being carried on with Muhammad Hakim at Kabul. It was hoped that he would lead an army into India, so that the imperial power might be attacked on two sides at once, and that then the country would rise in support of an orthodox prince. Influential men at court had been drawn into the conspiracy; and the chief of these was Shah Mansur. It was not long before Akbar gained full knowledge of the plot. Letters of Shah Mansur to Muhammad Hakim were intercepted, and he was suspended from his post. But soon after, Akbar having meanwhile taken preventive measures against the conspirators, he was reinstated. Shah Mansur seized the opportunity to renew his treasonable correspondence, which again fell into the emperor's hands. This time he was put in prison.

A tentative invasion of the Punjab by his brother, though unsuccessful, and the knowledge of so much secret disloyalty at his court, convinced Akbar that he had better make an end of this business. And he set about it with uncommon care. He felt his throne to be in serious danger, and he went about armed on all occasions.

Aquaviva and Monserrate were a good deal troubled in their minds. Knowing the great hostility they had provoked among the Muslims, and feeling that they had contributed to the emperor's danger by winning such marked favour, they sought him out at the beginning of these troubles and asked if he wished to dismiss them. Akbar, on the contrary, reproached them for being homesick. As soon as the campaign was decided on, they asked to be allowed to join the expedition. He said No; they were men of peace, and divine meditation was more suitable for such than the hardships of war: they were to be lodged with his mother. But next day he came into the schoolroom where the young Murad was at lessons with his tutor, and Monserrate was told to prepare for a journey. 'You are going with me.'

Hence it was that a Jesuit priest accompanied a Mogul army into Afghanistan, though it is a wonder that he returned alive, for on the Khyber Pass he would certainly have been stoned to death for his denunciation of the Prophet before a crowd of angry Muslims, had not fear of Akbar restrained them. Happily he returned safely, with all his notes, and we have the good fortune of seeing Akbar conduct a campaign through the eyes of a trained and intelligent observer, who set down many details which the Persian chronicles assume to be familiar to a reader. An observer, too, who is keenly interested in practical and military affairs, nor wholly absorbed like the saintly and absent-minded Aquaviva in his religious mission.

Since in this brief sketch there can be no room for more than a brief summary of Akbar's wars, let us take advantage of Monserrate's notes on this campaign to describe it a little more fully.

When Muhammad Hakim took courage to invade the Punjab, Akbar took no notice. He thought as much of him, it appears, 'as an eagle of a mosquito.' He merely sent a friendly message to invite him to the capital. But Muhammad Hakim was too wary to put himself in his brother's hands. His apprehensions rose to acute alarm when he heard that Akbar had given orders for a hunting expedition. For this was Akbar's invariable first move in a campaign. When the order for a hunt was given, it was time for his enemies to tremble.

And Muhammad Hakim took at once to flight, helter-skelter, over the mountains, losing hundreds of his horsemen at the crossing of the great rivers. Akbar, however, was not content with this cheap triumph. He was determined to make an end of the trouble. There was not only Kabul to be reckoned with, but Bengal; and not only these but traitors at home.

Sending his foster-brother, Mirza Aziz Koka, to Bengal to put down the rebellion, he prepared for the march on Kabul with unusual care. But first he released Shah Mansur. He disguised the fact that he knew all about the conspiracy, and professed that the able Finance Minister had been imprisoned only on suspicion. Shah Mansur was to join the expedition.

Nothing was left to chance. The new governors of Bengal and of Gujerat were provided with adequate armies; garrisons were left in the principal cities. The emperor took with him his two eldest sons, Salim and Murad, and Murad's tutor, Monserrate; some of his principal wives, and a quantity of gold and silver and other stores carried on elephants and camels. Then the usual orders for a hunting expedition were announced, and the immense white pavilion of the emperor was set up four miles from the capital. The tents of the great nobles and of the troops were disposed about it in the traditional manner of the Mongols, no doubt in the order first thought out by Jinghiz Khan. No Roman camp was more orderly or planned with more regular routine. Markets were attached to each division of the army. At night a cresset blazed from the top of a high mast, to guide stragglers and to be a rallying point in case of disturbance.

On 8th February 1581 the advance began. Two days had been given to hunting with cheetahs; the hunt being used as a sort of rehearsal, to familiarise all the units of the army with their proper functions and relative positions.

The distance of each day's march was carefully measured, for these measurements were found to be very useful in computing the areas of provinces and calculating the time of journeys. To the rhythm of a single drum, beaten at short intervals, the army, with all its elaborate appointments, moved forward like a stately procession—elephants, mounted archers, pikemen and light cavalry; for Akbar dispensed with all but a small force of infantry on this campaign. In any case, it was always the mounted forces that he relied on in his battles.

There was much to arouse the Jesuit's astonishment. For one thing, the army seemed at first remarkably small; but soon it increased so rapidly that it seemed to cover the earth. Then, with so great a host to feed, there was the cheapness of the grain: but this was the result of Akbar's foresight. Agents had been sent on beforehand to bring in provisions from all sides, and the merchants, if they sold cheaply, were promised exemption from taxes.

The frontier once passed, a different order was observed. Heralds were sent on in advance to the petty rajahs of the country to be traversed with conciliating messages and warning against resistance. Provisions would be paid for. And the army continued to be well fed. Water, however, was a necessity to be considered: and avoiding the plains, Akbar led his troops among the mountains, where the streams were abundant. Sappers and gangs of workmen were sent ahead to make a road. Akbar's chief military engineer, Muhammad Qasim Khan, was in charge of these. He had been, as a matter of fact, one of the conspirators, and Akbar knew it: but Akbar knew how to treat men, and the engineer came to think that he did better to be on the emperor's side. Bridges of boats were also made across the rivers, and officers stationed on the banks to see that they were not endangered by overcrowding. Outposts and scouts preceded and flanked the advance. Severe discipline was enforced throughout the army.

Near Sonpat a letter from Muhammad Hakim to Shah Mansur arrived and was intercepted. It was the third time that treasonable letters had been seized. There is some doubt whether these last letters were not forged: there is little or no doubt about the treason. Shah Mansur was again put under arrest. A few days later he was taken out by a guard, accompanied by the emperor and his generals. A halt was called. Abul Fazl was ordered to recite before those assembled all the benefits conferred on Shah Mansur since the obscure clerkship of his boyhood. He was then confronted with his own correspondence, and the proofs of his treason, and hanged upon a tree. The emperor returned to the camp with a sad countenance; whether because severity was distasteful to him or because he had lost so able a financier, no one knew. The army received the news with acclamation. The conspiracy, they felt, was cut off at the root. Muhammad Hakim, when he heard the news, knew that all was over, and began to think how he should make peace.

Violent storms now rendered the roads impassable and compelled a halt. As soon as the weather cleared the one European with the army saw for the first time the distant snows of the Himalayas. Though well occupied in observing and making notes of the countries passed through and their inhabitants, the Jesuit did not neglect his duty to his Order, and often engaged in religious discussions with both Muslims and Hindus; as it seemed to himself, with some success. Nor did he lose sight of the main object of the Jesuit mission, to convert the emperor: and judging it to be a propitious moment when news came that Muhammad Hakim had finally retired to Kabul, Monserrate, anxious that the emperor should not forget what he had been taught already, drew up an account of the Passion of Christ and handed it to him. The expedition had now reached the banks of the Indus, which, being impassable at that season except by boat, held up the advance for fifty days till sufficient boats could be collected; and Akbar had leisure for the discussions in which he delighted, as well as for his usual amusements of hunting and games. He showed a lively interest, as before, in the Gospel story, but, as before, showed no signs of real conversion. Then he asked the priest whether he should pursue Muhammad Hakim. Monserrate replied: 'Stay where you are, and do not pursue; for he is your Highness's brother. The glory of mercy is greater than the glory of vengeance.' Akbar applauded this answer: none the less, policy determined him to teach his brother a lesson, though he felt no vindictiveness towards him. He now sent the young Prince Murad forward in advance with several thousand cavalry and five hundred elephants. On this and on other occasions Monserrate was disconcerted by Akbar's superstitions and apparent respect for the soothsayers' predictions and choice of lucky days. But two days after his young pupil's departure, the emperor sent for the Father and spent many hours of the night questioning him not only on religious matters but on the geography of Europe. From the relative positions on the globe of Portugal and of India, they passed suddenly to a long discussion on celibacy and marriage and a spiritual offspring; and so to the Last Judgment, and thence to the Koran, when Abul Fazl broke in with questions on the Law and the Gospel; and though the emperor confused the Second and Third Persons of the

Trinity, Monserrate forbore to correct him, since the night was already nearing dawn.

But nothing seemed to weary Akbar: the next morning he would be up betimes, hunting, working in the carpenters' shops, giving innumerable orders, overseeing everything.

Meanwhile Muhammad Hakim, thoroughly alarmed, was pining to make terms of peace. But his uncle Faridun Khan, who hated Akbar, and whose superior force of character and ability intimidated him, derided the Mogul army as a scanty herd of infidels and idolaters, and stiffened him into some sort of resistance. Akbar therefore pursued his march. But the crossing of the Indus was only compassed with great difficulty and consumed a long time. Not only was the supply of boats inadequate, but the crossing was twice countermanded, to Monserrate's disgust, because of unfavourable omens. However at last the army was got across. Akbar halted on the further side till the passage was completed, spending his time in the workshops and in religious debates. Soon Peshawar was reached: and here news was brought of an attack on Prince Murad's force, in which the enemy had been repulsed but not before the Mogul ranks had been severely shaken. It was only the personal courage of

the twelve-year-old commander and the arrival
of reinforcements that prevented a check from
becoming a defeat. Murad had employed the
traditional Mogul tactics, and the cavalry was
drawn up in three divisions, right, centre, and
left, and in crescent formation; behind the
cavalry were the infantry, and behind the infantry the elephants. We learn from Monserrate that the elephants were ticklish beasts to
manage in battle: there was always a danger
of their doing less injury to the enemy than to
their own side. They terrified at first, but had
no terrors for horses when accustomed to the
sight of them: and when hurt they made no
distinction between friend and foe.

Akbar hastened on to Kabul by forced
marches on hearing the news, but left a strong
force to guard the passage of the Indus. Prince
Salim followed him with the rear-guard. The
army crossed the Khyber Pass, not without great
difficulty in spite of the labours of the sappers
and workmen. When on 9th August Akbar
entered Kabul, the capital of his grandfather
Babur, it was found that Muhammad Hakim
had fled to the loftiest and most inaccessible
mountain he could find.

Seven days only were spent at Kabul. Akbar
issued a proclamation assuring the safety of the

inhabitants: he did not war on civilians. He was elated at sitting on the throne of his father and grandfather, and happy in the success of his campaign. To him now came his sister, interceding for her brother and imploring that he might be restored to his kingdom now that he repented of his folly. Akbar's answer was to give the province into her charge, being assured of her loyalty and tact, and because he loved her. As for Muhammad Hakim, he wished never to hear his name again; he cared not a straw whether he lived at Kabul or elsewhere. Only he advised his sister to warn him not to resume his intrigues. Otherwise he would find the emperor not so inclined to clemency. Akbar could easily starve him into surrender; but he forbore to do so. Matters being thus arranged, he prepared to depart. On the first day of December Akbar re-entered Fatehpur-Sikri.

Monserrate was impressed on this campaign by Akbar's prudence and foresight, his states-manship and his clemency. These qualities are apparent; but from a military point of view one is also struck by the elaborate and un-wieldy paraphernalia with which the army was encumbered. However, Akbar knew his busi-ness, and adapted his methods of warfare to the enemy he was to encounter. The second

Gujerat campaign shows that, when need called, he could strike with unexampled swiftness. Then, speed and surprise were essential. In the Kabul campaign the enemy to be attacked seemed in himself hardly worthy of the immense care with which the expedition was prepared and the scale on which it was launched. But the circumstances were such that failure would have been fatal, not only to Akbar's army but to his throne and dynasty. Hence the great precautions taken; which, moreover, were indispensable for an army advancing into mountainous country, so advantageous to the defence. Akbar could apparently afford to advance in a leisurely manner with his imposing host, though an active and able antagonist might well have brought him to disaster.

XIII

WHEN, at the gates of Kabul, Monserrate offered
the emperor his congratulations, the Jesuit comments on Akbar's pleasure, with the surmise
that, being greedy of glory, he hoped that
through him his fame would reach Spain. In
fact Akbar, now much occupied with formu-
lating a new religion which was to unify all his
subjects, was also bent on establishing some sort
of contact with the Powers of Europe. How
serious he was, we cannot tell. But he now
decided to send a mission to Europe, with the
rather fantastic proposition that he should join
Portugal against the Turks. He also wrote a
letter to the Pope. He insisted that Monserrate
should be one of the envoys; Sayyid Muzaffar
was to go with him. But what was to become
of Aquaviva? It was arranged that he should
stay behind and take over the tutorship of the
young Murad in Monserrate's place. Neither
of the Jesuits was happy, though they felt
obliged to acquiesce. The embassy to Europe
never got farther than Goa. Sayyid Muzaffar,
who had from the first been most reluctant, de-

serted and hid himself somewhere in the Deccan. The embassy was postponed; and Monserrate was ordered by his Father Provincial to Abyssinia. On the voyage he was imprisoned by the Arabs; returned to India, and died, worn out, in 1600.

As for Aquaviva, he felt that the whole mission, which he and Monserrate had undertaken with such splendid expectations, was a failure, and he longed to get away. He was now sure that the emperor would never be converted. In vain did Abul Fazl plead that Akbar, who loved to have foreigners at his court, liked the Fathers above all other foreigners; in vain did he point to the extraordinary reverence with which he had treated their Bible, far surpassing the respect he paid to a Koran presented to him on the same day, 'though it was far more richly bound.' Aquaviva had only a mournful smile for such trivialities. Sweet-tempered as ever— even the Hindus called him 'the Angel'—he was firm in his resolve to go. And at last, a year or more after Akbar's return from Kabul, he had his way and persuaded the Father Provincial to recall him. Very loth, the emperor allowed him to depart and gave him a guard for escort. He arrived at Goa in the month of May 1583. Two months later he was murdered by a Hindu mob (true, their temples had been destroyed by the priests, and they had some cause to be enraged) and attained the martyrdom he had so long desired.

Though the embassy to Europe came to nothing, in the same year, 1583, there was a movement on the part of Europe, and this time from England. Queen Elizabeth addressed a letter to Akbar—his renown had already reached our remote island—as 'the most invincible and most mightie prince.' It was the first communication between the two countries, afterwards to be so intimately connected. John Newbery, a London merchant, was the envoy chosen: but there is no record of his reception. Seventeen years later Elizabeth sent another envoy, John Mildenhall, to seek trading privileges equal with those of the Portuguese. He was graciously received, but when Akbar consulted the Jesuits about the matter they were in a great rage and denounced all Englishmen as spies and thieves. Mildenhall, on his side, accused the Jesuits of bribing people at court to oppose him. His accusations may have been unfounded, but the whole episode has a sordid flavour; how different an atmosphere it breathes from that of the early colloquies between Akbar and Aquaviva!

But this is to anticipate. We must return to the state of things in 1582.

The discussions in the House of Worship had been languishing for some time. Soon after the end of the Kabul campaign they ceased altogether. There came a day when Akbar found there the Jesuit Fathers, but nobody to question or oppose them in the empty hall. Recognising failure, he had the building destroyed.

All those impassioned disputations had come to nothing, had brought no agreement, but rather embittered differences. Still Akbar was tenacious of his ideas. It seemed now that if anything further was to be done in the domain of religion the initiative must come from himself.

Akbar's ultimate ambition was to solder India into unity. His dream was to bring the whole vast country under one rule, whether by force of arms or the attraction of his prestige. Not to conquer and overrun after the manner of his Central Asian ancestors, and leave an empire that, founded on force alone, would inevitably shake to pieces after his death; but by a more gradual process, adding province to province, establishing a firm and just administration. He, a foreigner and a Muhammadan born, meant to identify himself with India.

But then, as ever, diversity of religion presented itself as the inveterate difficulty and obstacle. Could it be possible to formulate a creed that should unite all men of good will?

He had explored all the faiths known to him; he had found good in all, and good men professing each. Probably the attraction he found in Christianity, apart from the attraction he felt to the Gospel, was just the possibility of its proving a religion that, new to all his subjects alike, might be accepted by all. He soon saw, when he came to close quarters with Christian priests, how idle such an expectation, if he ever entertained it, must be. The mutual hostility of Muslim and Christian was too fierce and deep: nor did the Hindus show any of the affability shown by the Japanese in the sixteenth century to Christian doctrine before political arrogance, ambition, and intrigue undid the victories of missionary fervour. Where, then, was he to turn? He had adopted, in part at least, each of the chief religions of India. But none wholly satisfied his spirit, and the idea of unity still haunted his mind.

Shaikh Mubarak, that learned and unorthodox theologian, father of his dear friend Abul Fazl, had once dropped a seed in his mind. He had appealed to him to become not only the

temporal but the spiritual ruler of his empire.
The seed germinated. Akbar, a mystic at heart,
who never could identify religion with the
forms it inhabited, began to see the needed
symbol of spiritual unity in himself. After all,
why not? He alone symbolised the unity of all
the divers elements which made up the empire.
There was one God, one object of worship for
all the various jarring creeds and sects. Akbar,
responsible for all, was the earthly represen-
tative of that divine idea. There was no one
else who would serve. So at last in 1582 the
long-cherished idea came to fruit, and he pro-
mulgated the new Divine Faith which was to
weld all the antagonisms of the creeds into one.

It was the year after his return from the
Kabul campaign. The Bengal rebellion no
longer caused anxiety; treachery at home had
been firmly dealt with; fear of invasion was
over. Akbar felt secure, and powerful enough
to override all opposition. He called a General
Council and imparted his views to it. After
dwelling on the discord which so many different religions produced in politics, he continued: 'We ought therefore to bring them all
into one, but in such fashion that they should be
both "one" and "all"; with the great advantage
of not losing what is good in one religion, while

gaining whatever is better in another. In that way, honour would be rendered to God, peace would be given to the people, and security to the empire.'

The Divine Faith was, of course, a failure, and destined to failure. In religious societies toleration is no virtue, it is the despised off-spring of lukewarmness or indifference. A creed so simple was obvious to the reproach of vagueness and emptiness. Most unfortunate of all, Akbar's assumption of a mystic rôle as 'Head of the Church' laid him open to every kind of worldly suspicion. But the dream was not an ignoble dream. Those who have seen in it merely self-aggrandisement or astuteness surely misread Akbar's character.

The religion, which was to have united all, pleased none. Moreover, such is the weakness of human nature, Akbar, who had revolted so far from the intolerance of his ancestral creed, now impaired his own toleration by invidious ordinances against Muhammadan practices. Just as champions of international goodwill are often found to exempt their own country from a universal benevolence, and to look on it alone with a malignant eye, so this descendant of conquerors who had treated all alien creeds with fierce contempt was warped into oppressing, of all faiths, the faith in which he was bred. As the years went on, his dislike of Muhammad and his whole religious system became more bitter. In 1595 the Jesuit Pinheiro finds in Lahore not a mosque, not a Koran: what mosques remained had been turned into stables. 'The King has made a sect of his own, and makes himself out to be a prophet. He has already many people who follow him, but it is all for money which he gives them. He adores God, and the Sun, and is a Hindu: he follows the sect of the Jains.' Thirteen years, then, after the promulgation of the 'Divine Faith,' we find Akbar still pursuing his eclectic modes of religious observance, while the new religion, centring in the emperor's person, is evidently making little way; and perhaps unconsciously avenging its failure on the Muhammadans, who had always opposed the vagaries of his spirit.

How deeply Akbar felt the disappointment of his hopes, we do not know: perhaps he was self-deceived and magnified his success with time-servers and flatterers; he certainly seems to have persuaded himself that divine powers vested themselves in royalty—a persuasion not unknown to Europe. It was in any case plain that he had not the genius of a religious leader. But at least the external and material unity of his empire was an aim he could still pursue, and in that domain he was no fumbler.

XIV

THE empire was still far from commensurate
with its ruler's ambition. All the great region
to the south was outside his sway, and to the
north and west there were kingdoms that he
coveted.

It was to Kashmir and Sind that he first
turned his attention. Kashmir was annexed.
But not without grievous losses. The emperor
no longer conducted his campaigns himself;
and it was a weakness in him as a ruler that he
did not always choose his lieutenants wisely.
The three generals sent on this campaign quar-
relled, as was not unnatural; for one of them
was Birbal, an intimate and trusted friend of
Akbar's, it is true, but a musician, a poet, a
jester, rather than a soldier or commander. An
ill-advised march resulted in a surprise attack
in a mountain pass. Akbar could bear the loss
of eight thousand men more calmly than the
loss of Birbal, who was killed in the engage-
ment: Birbal, his dear Birbal, his merry com-
panion, whose voice as he talked or sang in the
evenings verses of his own composing, was still

in his ears: Birbal, for whom he had built so beautiful a house at Fatehpur-Sikri: Birbal, the one Hindu who had embraced the emperor's new religion of the Divine Faith. But Akbar was now coming to that time of life when the friends of a man's youth begin to die, and he has to bear the blows of Time as best he may.

Kashmir was subdued, and in the spring of 1589 Akbar left Lahore and arrived at Srinagar; thence he moved to Kabul, and there learned of two other deaths which touched him nearly: the death of Bhagwan Das, the first of the Rajput princes to join the Mogul, the brave soldier who had fought side by side with Akbar at Chitor and in Gujerat: and the death of Todar Mall, the simple clerk who rose to be prime minister and was one of Akbar's most trusted generals.

With the annexation of Sind in 1591 by a campaign conducted by that able son of the Protector Bairam Khan, Abdurrahim, whom Akbar had welcomed and cherished as a child after the death of his father, the schemes of conquest were for the time completed. In the following year Orissa in the east was annexed. Four years later, Baluchistan and Kandahar were added to the empire.

The Deccan remained. The emperor may well have thought that the prestige of his name was now so formidable that the rulers of the Southern Kingdoms would acknowledge his suzerainty without the laborious effort of protracted campaigns; and it has been thought that his real aim was not so much the subjugation of those regions as the securing of a vantage point from which to proceed against the Portuguese and drive them from their settlements on the coast. He was now again in touch with the Portuguese; for at his request a second Jesuit mission arrived at the court in 1591, and though this was abortive, he succeeded in persuading a third mission to be sent three years later. The head of this third mission, Father Jerome Xavier, was to remain at court, with Akbar and with his successor, for no less than twenty-three years, and to enjoy as much familiarity with the emperor as Aquaviva and Monserrate. But hardly the same trust and friendship. Aquaviva and Monserrate were honest and devoted men to whom the cause of Christianity among the infidels was everything. The later Jesuit envoys were perhaps equally zealous; but with their zeal for the faith was mingled a keen sense for political and commercial advantage. In the end all three missions failed of their first object, the emperor's conversion.

Akbar's opening move in his designs on the Deccan was to send four envoys to the four kingdoms or sultanates with which he would first have to deal. The most important of them, from his point of view, as being the most accessible, were Khandesh, of which Burhanpur was the capital, and Ahmadnagar.

When the envoys returned, after a prolonged absence, their news was not favourable. The fact that the ruler of Ahmadnagar sent a meagre and inadequate present was considered a sufficient motive for declaring war. Abdurrahim, the conqueror of Sind, was appointed general; but unfortunately there was associated with him in joint command the young prince Murad: and inevitable quarrels, ensued. Murad, whose intelligence and docility as a boy had so impressed his tutor, Monserrate, was already beginning to be enslaved to drink and drugs. It was the family vice. Babur had indulged in long bouts of drunkenness—the sight of a field of flowers or a beautiful sunset was an excuse for celebrating his joy in it—though his strong will enabled him to forswear drink altogether at need. Humayun had sapped his

constitution by opium. Even Akbar was sometimes stupefied by opiate drinks, though he
never allowed the vice to be his master: but all
his three sons were drunkards.

Siege was laid to Ahmadnagar, which was defended by Chand Bibi as regent, one of the
heroic women who, like Durgavati, the first
victim of Akbar's ambition, shine out in Indian
history. (Chand Bibi hawking in the plains is
a favourite subject of the Indian painters.)
And so successful was the defence that the
Moguls were compelled to accept terms quite
unworthy of the imperial prestige: the treaty
was signed early in 1596. In the following year
Murad was superseded in his command.

Meanwhile Akbar remained at Lahore, griev-
ously disappointed with the failure of his second son, and now beginning to be yet more
disturbed by the insubordinate attitude of his
eldest, Prince Salim. There were other troubles. For three years a terrible famine, followed by plague, devastated the whole of
Northern India. So accustomed was the country to these periodic visitations, so resigned its
inhabitants, that the famine is but casually noticed by native historians. The roads were
blocked with dead bodies; men were reduced
to eating their own kind. Relief measures were

undertaken, but were quite inadequate to the famine's vast extent.

The Fathers doubtless decided that such calamities were judgments of Heaven on the emperor for his failure to listen whole-heartedly to their counsels: they found some consolation in baptizing all the abandoned infants they could find.

They record with still more satisfaction a disaster that seemed to be a personal chastisement of the emperor by the wrath of God. For on Easter Day, 1597, there was a sudden fire at Lahore where Akbar was celebrating the festival of the sun. A great part of the palace was consumed, with its treasure and costly furniture, so that the molten gold and silver streamed into the streets.

While the palace was rebuilding, Akbar retired to Kashmir, taking with him Jerome Xavier and one of his companions; they were enchanted with the climate of the hills, the flowering trees and the verdure, the orchards, springs, and streams.

But by now things were going so ill in the Deccan that the presence of the emperor was needed if they were not to end in an ignominious failure.

In May 1599 Prince Murad died of delirium
tremens. In July Akbar left Prince Salim in
charge of Agra and began to move south. In
the following year he occupied Burhanpur.
Prince Daniyal was ordered to take the city of
Ahmadnagar, hitherto so bravely and effec-
tively defended by Chand Bibi. But internal
dissensions now arose among the besieged:
Chand Bibi was murdered by an insurgent mob
or perhaps forced to take poison: and in August
1600 the town was taken. So far the young
Daniyal seemed to promise well: and Akbar
destined him to be the future ruler of the conquered Deccan. But Murad had shown equal
promise, and Daniyal was to go the way of
Murad. Moreover, the Deccan was not yet
conquered.

The country of Khandesh trusted to its great
fortress of Asirgarh. Asirgarh was famous as
the strongest and most formidable fortress in all
India, probably in the whole world. It was imperative that it should be taken, for it commanded the pass and high road between the
Deccan and Hindostan. But how? The natural strength of Asirgarh was enormous. Rising
nine hundred feet above the plain, the huge
mass of rock was enclosed by a triple line of
fortifications. The plateau on the summit, a

space of sixty acres, contained an unfailing supply of water from wells and reservoirs. There were stocks of provisions calculated to support the garrison for ten years, although, according to Abul Fazl, 34,000 persons marched out from the gates at the final capitulation, and 25,000 had died of pestilence during the siege. These figures are surely exaggerations. Except in two places Asirgarh was surrounded by sheer cliffs. The methods employed at Chitor, the approach by sap and mine, were useless here. And while the Mogul artillery was weak, the defenders had vast reserves of ammunition for their thirteen hundred guns; and, moreover, the officers of the gunners were Portuguese.

The siege began in April under the command of Abul Fazl; but it was soon made apparent that little progress would be made by direct attack. A singular custom prevailed in Asirgarh that seven princes of the royal blood should always dwell there, ready to assume the king-ship in turn. The present king was called Bahadur. But the commander of the defences was, strange to say, an Abyssinian, now old and going blind, but of an heroic temper and firm will. In May Bahadur offered terms to the besiegers, but they were not acceptable, and were refused.

The story of the capture of Asirgarh is obscure. The events are recorded by Abul Fazl, who was in command of the siege, and by the French author Du Jarric, who founded his narrative on Jesuit accounts. Jerome Xavier was present at the siege, so it is natural to think that his notes were used. Yet the two accounts are impossible to reconcile. Vincent Smith takes Du Jarric's story as literally true; but Mr. Payne, the English editor of Du Jarric, shows that Vincent Smith's accusations of falsehood on the part of Abul Fazl and other native historians are largely unfounded. Was there a pestilence destroying thousands of the defenders? It is not even mentioned by Du Jarric, but it could hardly have been an entire invention. Whether on account of this calamity or of the capture in November of a fort commanding the main defences, or of both, Bahadur was disheartened and sent an envoy to Abul Fazl, who sent him on to Akbar. Further negotiations brought a young man, Muqarrab Khan, the son of the Abyssinian governor, down to the camp, offering that if the fortress and country were restored and prisoners released, Bahadur would submit. These terms were granted. Bahadur then asked that Aziz Koka should take his hand and escort him to the emperor's presence. Bahadur came down and prostrated himself. Once in Akbar's hands, he was not allowed to return.

But the fort was not yet taken, and the old Abyssinian governor was in no mood to yield. Akbar, however, was impatient. The news he had of Prince Salim at Agra was disturbing: his presence was urgently needed in the north. He had sounded the Jesuits as to the possibility of getting artillery from the Portuguese, but they had refused to help him. Since heavy guns were wanting, he was obliged to fall back on bribery. Assiduous bribing had its effect; most of the defenders were won over. In vain the old Abyssinian assembled all the princes of the royal blood and asked which of them would accept the throne and defend the honour of his fathers. Not one answered. 'Would to God you were women!' he cried. Just then Muqar-rab came up from the camp with a message from Akbar. His father turned on him: 'May God not show me thy face! Go down to Bahadur and follow him!' The young man, overcome with shame, went back to the camp, and in the presence of Abul Fazl and the Mogul chiefs stabbed himself in the belly and died. The old man his father, seeing that there was no more hope, bathed, had his shroud brought him, distributed alms, and took poison. The defenders, having got their gold, decided to open the gates; but first they stipulated that they should have a letter from Bahadur approving their action, to cover their disgrace. Bahadur was forced to consent. In the early days of 1601 the keys of this impregnable fortress were surrendered.

The lives of the garrison were spared. It is somewhat amusing to read that Akbar was greatly angered when the Portuguese officers of artillery confessed that they had become Muhammadans. He abused them as apostates. It was Xavier who interceded for them, and before long had succeeded in reconverting them to Christianity.

Asirgarh had been taken, but the method of its capture could not redound to Akbar's glory. The grand scheme of subduing the Deccan was indeed to prove abortive: his career of conquest had reached its term.

XV

IF the Deccan disappointed Akbar's last ambition, there were other and worse blows preparing for the last decade of his life, blows at his very heart.

There had been a time when all the triumphs of his early manhood seemed vain because he had no son, no heir. How earnestly he had prayed for a son, how eagerly welcomed the hermit's prophecy, how exulted when the prophecy came true! And how he had loved his first-born, Salim! Yet it was this beloved son who was to deal him the cruellest stroke of his life.

Prince Salim found that his father had lived long enough. Was he never to mount the throne himself? He grew more and more arrogant and impatient. Akbar was well aware of his son's rebellious feelings. He had even suspected Salim of attempting to poison him. Yet Salim was still dear, and there was no one else to succeed him. Murad, the docile, intelligent pupil of Monserrate, who as a boy had shown such courage in the field, had become a hopeless drunkard and was dead. Daniyal, the youngest, who had been destined by Akbar to be the governor of the conquered Deccan, was going, in spite of all efforts to prevent him, the same way; his passion for strong drink amounted to madness; when he could get it in no other way he had it smuggled in to him in the barrels of soldiers' muskets; it was before long to destroy him in delirium. Salim was tainted with the same vice, but had it more under control. He was savagely cruel in the punishments he inflicted, yet genial when he chose. He was not without ability, and he was capable both of feeling and of inspiring strong affection. He was now, in 1600, thirty-one years of age.

While Akbar was still in the south, Salim decided to show his independence. What if he should seize Agra, with all its fabulous treasure! The thought inflamed him, but his nerve failed. He moved on to Allahabad. His grandmother, who was devoted to him, had gone out from Agra to meet him, for she knew of his intentions, and earnestly wished to dissuade him. But, to her grief and chagrin, he avoided her. Arrived at Allahabad, he assumed sovereign powers, seizing whole provinces and allotting them as fiefs to his followers.

Akbar, returned from the Deccan, heard that his son was advancing on Agra with thirty thousand horsemen. He sent urgent messages to stop him, and appointed him governor of Bengal and Orissa. Salim retired to Allahabad, but abated nothing of his pretensions, negotiating with his father as king with king, making large and insolent demands. He even had his own coinage minted, and to goad his father to greater anger, sent specimens of the coins to Akbar.

About the middle of 1602 Abul Fazl, in supreme command in the Deccan, received from the emperor a despatch informing him of the prince's rebellion. Abul Fazl replied in a confident tone that he would soon bring the rebel to heel, and forthwith set out of Agra. He was warned of a possible ambush, but insisted on taking only a small retinue. Later in the journey he was again warned by a fakir of intended treachery, but again took no notice and refused a bodyguard. On a morning in August the little party were preparing to march when five hundred armed horsemen suddenly appeared and blocked the road. They surrounded and overpowered the escort after a brief struggle; Abul Fazl was killed by a spear-thrust, and his head struck off.

Bir Singh, who commanded the murderers, sent the head to Prince Salim, who gloated over the sight and exulted in the death of his father's dearest friend. For it was Salim who had contrived the murder and hired Bir Singh to do it. He was afraid of Abul Fazl's influence with his father; knew him hostile to himself, and had resolved that he should never arrive at the capital. Afterwards, when he was emperor, he justified the act and congratulated himself on his good luck in that 'by the grace of God' Bir Singh's country was so conveniently on the route of the returning minister.

That he should lose his great friend, his right hand in the ruling of his empire, 'the King's Jonathan,' as the Jesuits called him, was sorrow enough for Akbar; but that his friend should be brutally murdered by the hireling agent of his own son was a grief unspeakable. The emperor's anger even surpassed his grief. For three days he secluded himself, against all custom, from the public gaze. And he sent out orders to search for Bir Singh and kill him wherever found. The hunt failed to capture the quarry. Bir Singh was pursued so closely as to get a wound, but succeeded in escaping into the territory of Gwalior. Akbar raged in vain.

This was a most unhappy time. The emperor was sore and bitter in his heart; at one time minded to march against his rebel son and crush him, at another shrinking from open civil war. It was rumoured that he intended to make Salim's son, Khusru, his heir, instead of his father. And there were powerful supporters of this project, notably Rajah Man Singh, brother of Salim's wife. Khusru is described by the English Terry as 'a gentleman of very lovely presence' and very popular. His youthful promise shone by comparison with his father's tyrannical cruelties and fits of wild intemperance.

At last a kind of reconciliation was brought about. The widow of Bairam Khan, the Protector of Akbar's early years on the throne, Salima Begam, whom the emperor had married in his youth, journeyed to Allahabad and used all her persuasion to bring Salim to submission. In the spring of 1603 Salim consented to come to Agra. Salima was with him, and Akbar's mother, though nearing eighty, was easily persuaded by her to house the prince; she even went out a day's journey to meet him. Through her, too, father and son were at last induced to meet. Salim presented his father with a large sum in gold and seven hundred and seventy

elephants: at which Akbar was touched: he had
a passion for elephants. And he curbed his
feelings, and behaved with ceremonious polite-
ness, even placing his own turban on Salim's
head. The supporters of the young Khusru
were disconcerted; for the act was a symbolic
acknowledgment by the emperor of his heir.

But it was a hollow reconciliation between
these two estranged spirits. The blood of Abul
Fazl flowed between them. Akbar desired his
son to undertake a military expedition in Rajputana; and Salim, having no such intention,
only asked for more and more men and money.
After futile negotiations, Salim, now residing at
Fatehpur-Sikri, asked permission to retire to
Allahabad. Thither in November of this year,
1603, he returned, and resumed his former
show of royal state, and held a separate court.
With all his ferocities, Salim showed now, as in
former years, a great interest in the Christian
religion and paid much flattering attention to
the Jesuits; in so much that they seriously
hoped for his definite conversion. He presented them with a silver image of the infant
Jesus for their church. In fact, so far as external behaviour showed—for who can tell
what really was in Salim's heart?—he had 'far
greater regard for the Fathers, and for the

Christian religion, than the King.' Whatever his ulterior aim, he certainly desired to have the Jesuits and their influence on his side.

On one occasion Father Xavier found the prince busy in the curious operation of extracting copper from peacock's tails, as an antidote to poison. Poison was in the air. Akbar suspected Salim, and Salim suspected the adherents of his own son Khusru. This sinister distrust was to be the inveterate canker in the brilliant dynasty of the Moguls, son against father, brother against brother; the tragedy was to culminate with Shah Jahan imprisoned in his old age by his son Aurangzeb, who had destroyed his brothers to mount upon the throne.

In this atmosphere, heavy with suspicion, the estrangement continued and deepened. Akbar, brooding and chafing, heard of Salim's increasing pretensions with mounting anger. His son's assumption of the royal title was, according to the Jesuits, the crowning insolence which moved him to action. He ordered Salim to his presence; but afraid of putting himself in his father's power, and afraid of being superseded, as was now again the rumour, by Khusru, Salim turned a deaf ear to this command. Akbar, thoroughly aroused, at last determined to march with an army and compel submission.

Salim, on his part, rallied all his adherents and collected a force of equal magnitude. Civil war was about to break out.

Once more the queen-mother intervened. Hamida, who long ago as a slim girl of fourteen had half-unwillingly married the fugitive Humayun in the deserts of Sind, had shared all Akbar's fortunes and seen him grow from the adventurous boy, beset with dangers, to be the most potent and glorious of monarchs. But now her heart was with the grandson; she loved him dearly: and she foresaw how poor a chance he had, pitting his strength against the winner of a hundred battles. She implored Akbar to relent, and not march against his son. But Akbar had hardened his heart; he would not listen. She was overcome with grief, and, old and frail, became dangerously ill. The emperor was already on the march: the news was brought him: and though at first he thought her sickness was feigned, when it was confirmed beyond doubt he turned back in remorse to Agra. When he arrived his mother was worse, and in a few days she was dead. The body was conveyed to Delhi, to lie by the side of Humayun.

Akbar mourned for her after the Hindu fashion, shaving the hair of his head. It was not his only loss in this unhappy year (1604): for his youngest son, Daniyal, had died miserably in the spring, frustrating all his father's hopes for him. Sick with grief, Akbar had no heart to pursue his expedition; and negotiations were renewed. A skilful agent was employed to induce the prince to come before him as a supplicant, when all his offences would be forgiven.

In the end Salim was persuaded to submit. In continual dread of being superseded by his son, perhaps he decided that it was his safest course.

In November he arrived at Agra. He had marched with a large body of troops, but had left them at some distance from the city. Once more he brought gold and elephants as a present, though this time the elephants were only four hundred in number. The emperor received him publicly 'in a certain gallery' or verandah. Salim prostrated himself humbly before his father, who received him with many signs of affection, and then, taking him by the hand, he drew him apart into an inner room. Suddenly Akbar lost control of himself. His pent-up fury exploded. He slapped his son's face and bitterly reproached him, enumerating all his unfilial misdeeds. His anger was terrible.

Then with a sudden change of tone he mocked at his son for his folly in coming unarmed as a suppliant when he had a huge host of horsemen at his call. Salim, quite cowed, cast his eyes on the ground and answered with streaming eyes.

The scene ended with Salim's arrest. He was deprived of wine and opium, 'the hardest of punishments.' The prince was heartbroken. But soon his sisters and Akbar's wives came and comforted him with tears and sympathy. They went to and fro between him and the emperor, and made so pathetic a picture of his contrition and repentance that Akbar's heart, always inclined to mercy after the explosion of his wrath, was softened, and in a few days Salim was released and could solace his mortification again with wine.

Akbar's overmastering personality was never more signally manifested than in the quelling by his presence of his presumptuous son, who, apart from him, had been audacious to insolence both in word and act. Salim, while his father lived, gave no more serious trouble.

But Akbar's days were numbered. He had scarce a year more to live. A man of strong affections and great ambitions, he had been deeply wounded in both. The murder of Abul Fazl, the rebellion of Salim, the death of his mother, had made his heart sore with grief and anger. All his glory had turned to ashes. The ignoble and untimely deaths of his two younger sons had ruined long-cherished hopes, and the character of the eldest promised no auspicious future for his dynasty. Should he, after all, pass over Salim in favour of his grandson Khusru? Whether Akbar seriously considered this at the end we do not know; but certainly as soon as his fatal illness began, on 21st September 1605, the adherents of that youth began to plot in earnest. They resolved to arrest Salim on a day when he came back by water to pay his respects to the emperor. His boat had touched the steps of the landing at the fortress when he was warned of his danger; and so he escaped the conspirators. They gathered the great nobles together and debated the succession, but the claims of Khusru were strongly opposed, and in the end the plot failed.

Salim, who had so passionately desired his father's death, yet knew his father's greatness: he was torn with anxieties for the future, perhaps with some remorse for the past. He spent a whole night wandering about in sleepless disquietude. In the streets of the capital he, the heir to the throne, went about with the looks of a fugitive. Not till his father was actually dying did he dare to venture into Akbar's presence: or perhaps he was excluded: mutual suspicions still hung their clouds between son and father. In spite of Akbar's immensely strong constitution, the dysentery gained on him. Every small vexation now aggravated his illness. Yet towards the end he rallied. On 22nd October, a Saturday, Father Xavier and his fellow Jesuits were admitted to the sick-room, expecting a death-bed scene, and primed with admonitions on the state of the sufferer's soul, and were amazed to find him cheerful and merry among his courtiers. On the Monday, however, a change had taken place: when they asked for admittance they were refused. Akbar was dying: their opportunity was lost.

Prince Salim, assured of the support of the nobles, since he had sworn to maintain the faith of Islam and not to punish the adherents of Khusru, at last with a strong bodyguard came to the palace, and was ushered into his father's presence. He bowed and touched the ground with his forehead. Akbar had by now lost the power of speech; but he opened his eyes: he was conscious, and still, in the hour of death, commanding. He made signs to his son that he should place the imperial turban on his head, and then gird on the imperial sword, the sword of Humayun. Then with another silent gesture he signed to him to withdraw. Salim went swiftly out: he breathed freely: he lifted his head high: he heard the acclamations of the crowd and felt assured of his throne.

Only a few of his closest friends remained with the dying emperor. They repeated the creed of Muhammad, surrounding him with the atmosphere of the piety of his fathers and rebuilding the recollections of his infancy. But no sign of assent came from Akbar's lips. Only at intervals he tried to utter the name of God. Early in the morning of 27th October he expired.

The funeral, according to Muhammadan custom among the Sunni sect, was of the simplest. A gap was broken in the wall of the great red sandstone fort of Agra which Akbar himself had built, and through this the body was borne on the shoulders of Salim, now to be the Emperor Jahangir, and his son. A little procession followed it to the grave which had been prepared, at a distance of three miles. The few who wore mourning changed their clothes in the evening.

To the Jesuit observers these hurried and informal obsequies seemed scandalously maimed and slighted. Used to the pomp and ostentation which in Christendom accompany the dead, never more honoured in life than when the spirit has departed from the body: expecting the lofty catafalque, great burning candles, solemn music, sad apparel, prolonged and gorgeous ceremonial, the prayers of a vast and ordered multitude of mourners, they could not understand that the remains of so mighty a monarch should be committed to earth in so perfunctory a fashion unless it were from studied indifference or contempt. They were quick to moralise an epitaph; and 'Thus does the world,' one of them wrote, 'treat those from whom no good is to be hoped nor evil feared.' But they were ignorant that in Islam a contrary tradition prevailed, according to the precept of the Prophet that the dead should be carried quickly to the grave, for if it is good to make haste to put wickedness from one's shoulders, so it is good also that the blessed spirit should be hastened to its peace.

BIBLIOGRAPHICAL NOTE

THE following works may be consulted by those who
desire to explore the subject further:—

VINCENT SMITH. *Akbar, the Great Mogul.*
Clarendon Press. 2nd ed. 1919.

Col. G. B. MALLESON. *Akbar.* Rulers of India
series. Clarendon Press. 1890.

Monserrate's Commentary. (1) Latin text, edited
by Father H. HOSTEN. Calcutta, 1914. (2)
English translation, by J. S. HOYLAND, with
notes by S. W. BANERJEE. Milford: London
and Cuttack, 1922. (The original MS. only
came to light in Calcutta in 1906.)

PIERRE DU JARRIC, S.J. *Akbar and the Jesuits.*
Translated from Du Jarric's *Histoire* by C. H.
PAYNE. Routledge, 1926. (Contains full and
interesting notes, in which some of Vincent
Smith's misstatements are corrected.)

Akbar-namah. Translated by H. BEVERIDGE.
Bibliotheca Indica. Calcutta, 1897-1910.

Ain i Akbari. Translated by H. F. BLOCHMANN
and H. S. JARRETT. Bibliotheca Indica. Calcutta, 1873-1910.

India at the Death of Akbar, by W. H. MORE-
LAND, a study made from the economic point
of view, may also be mentioned.

Sir E. D. MACLAGAN's *The Jesuits and the Great
Mogul* is announced for early publication.

INDEX

INDEX

(1)